Knitting out of AFRICA

MARIANNE ISAGER

Inspired Sweater Designs

Editing: Ann Budd
Technical Editing: Lori Gayle
Translation: Carol Huebscher Rhoades
Design: Paulette Livers
Production: Dean Howes
Photo styling: Paulette Livers
Illustrations: Gayle Ford, Kirsten Toftegaard, and
                    Ase Lund Jensen
Photography: Joe Coca, unless otherwise noted
Proofreading and indexing: Nancy Arndt

Interweave Press LLC
201 East Fourth Street
Loveland, CO 80537-5655 USA
www.interweave.com

Printed and bound in China by Pimlico Book International

Library of Congress Cataloging-in-Publication Data

Isager, Marianne, 1954-
   Knitting out of Africa : inspired sweater
designs / Marianne Isager, author.
      p. cm.
   Includes index.
   ISBN 1-931499-98-5
   1. Knitting—Patterns. 2. Sweaters. I. Title.
   TT825.I83 2006
      746.43'2041—dc22
                  2005020185

10 9 8 7 6 5 4 3 2 1

ACKNOWLEDGMENTS

A sincere thank you to my dedicated and expert knitters who helped with the knitting and pattern instructions for this book:

Ulla Bohlin—Zaire and Kuba
Birthe Carlsen—Asante
Birthe Elkrog—Congo
Erna Engedal—Giraffe and Zebra
Kirsten Grønning Jensen—Sierra Leone
Mona Johansen—Mali, Arrowheads, Zimbabwe, Nigeria, and Zigzag
Kirsten Nielsen—Shoowa Vest
Ethel Sørensen—Shoowa
Inger Birthe Sørensen—African Domino

Also, thanks to the people who helped with source materials:

Hansjörg Mayer—photographs from the book *Shoowa Design*
Georges Meurant—Shoowa
Natural History Museum in Århus—loan of a skin for photography
Christopher Spring—African textiles

CONTENTS

INTRODUCTION

I have always been crazy for patterns. As soon as I learned to draw, I happily repeated a motif over and over. Although I didn't discover the joy of knitting until I was seventeen, from the very beginning I drew my own designs for garments and threw myself headlong into the most ambitious projects. My fascination for knitting grew as I discovered new techniques and the many different ways they could be applied.

Much of my inspiration comes from trips to museums and libraries. It was at the British Museum in London that I first became entranced by the rich tradition of African textile designs, ones that called out to be translated into knitted garments. For me, however, the excitement of designing doesn't come from simply copying patterns—it comes from developing a design that captures the feeling of a motif or pattern and adapting it to grace the body in a garment. I have traveled to Africa to experience firsthand the way the country's textiles reflect the landscape, wildlife, and cultural traditions. Unfortunately, I must disappoint those who would like to know the specific techniques or historical significance of the handcrafts that inspired the garments in this book. When possible, I've provided information about where a cloth or basket comes from, but I have little knowledge about the origins of these masterworks.

To make my knitted garments interesting and unusual, I've employed a variety of techniques—entrelac, slip-stitch knitting, stranded two-color knitting, intarsia, and double knitting. I've organized the sweaters in this book according to the technique I have used to represent the original textile.

ENTRELAC

Some years ago, I read an article in a Norweigian handwork magazine about a block pattern that was used long ago for the legs of socks. In Norway, the technique is called *neverkont,* a term that translates to "birch basket" and refers to a basket made of woven birch bark. In English, this technique is called entrelac. Entrelac knitting produces rows of blocks that are worked on the diagonal, and that alternate direction was a revelation for me: knitting does not have to be vertical or horizontal.

Entrelac is ideal for representing Shoowa textiles, which are woven from *Raphia farinifera* palm fibers, then embroidered and appliquéd. These decorative fabrics come from the western part of Congo, formerly known as Zaire. Shoowa textiles have historically been used in commerce and in burial ceremonies for wealthy citizens. The base fabric is woven on an upright frame loom, then embroidered with abstract patterns. Traditionally, Shoowa men cultivated the rafia palms and wove the base fabrics; the women dyed the cloth (a process that also softened the fibers), then embroidered or appliquéd them with designs that were specific to particular regions. Some patterns were named after the women who had created them, and a good designer was highly respected.

The garments named **Kuba, Zaire, Congo, Shoowa,** and **Shoowa Vest** are all inspired by these fascinating textiles. Except for the Shoowa pullover and vest, which are more logically worked in stranded two-color knitting, all include the entrelac technique. The **African Domino** cardigan and pullover are based on a variation of the entrelac technique, with the square shapes formed by working decreases in the center of a group of stitches.

SLIP-STITCH KNITTING

My inspiration for **Asante** came from a fabric printed by the Asante people in Ghana. After being woven, Asante fabrics are block-printed to create a collage of different patterns. Many of the pattern blocks are based on historic symbols for which they are named. To translate the play of pattern against pattern in knitting, I have used slip-stitch patterns that alternate two rows of a thick yarn with two rows of a thin yarn. Short-rows are used to maintain a consistent gauge between the stockinette-stitch and patterned sections.

INTARSIA KNITTING

Sierra Leone was inspired by a carpet woven in the eponymous country. The fabrics from this region are traditionally made up of 6" (15-cm) woven bands that are sewn together, often in a way that produces a checkerboard appearance. In knitting, this effect is easily achieved with intarsia, which allows the knitter to produce isolated blocks of color.

STRANDED TWO-COLOR KNITTING

Many African patterns can be interpreted in stranded two-color, or Fair Isle, knitting. This technique involves alternating two colors of yarn in a single row of knitting, and it allows for intricate geometric and abstract designs. The color patterns in *Mali, Arrowheads, Zimbabwe, Zigzag,* and *Nigeria* are achieved with stranded two-color knitting.

The cotton mud-dyed fabrics produced in the Bamana region of *Mali* inspired my sweater of the same name. Traditionally, these fabrics feature prominently in ceremonies of passage—birth, circumcision, marriage, and death. The cloth is woven on simple frame looms, then washed and plant-dyed to a weak yellow color. A pattern is drawn on the dried fabric and carefully filled in with a fermented mud compound rich in iron oxide that reacts with the yellow fabric to create a reddish color. The process can be repeated a number of times to create intricate patterns over large areas. The remaining yellow areas are then painted with a caustic soda to bleach them white and provide sharp contrast with the dyed areas. Some of the most common motifs are said to imitate crocodile skin, the double zigzag of cricket legs, fishbones, or small stars.

The combination of small arrows and triangles in *Arrowheads* comes from Mali cloth that was woven, embroidered, then plant-dyed. This intricate cloth is best represented by stranded two-color knitting.

East Africa is better known for basketry and fine wood carving than textiles. Throughout Zimbabwe, beautiful woven baskets are sold at roadside stands. The *Zimbabwe* sweater was inspired by a basket I purchased near the village of Bulawayo; the *Zigzag* sweater was inspired by a basket I bought near Lake Kariba on the Zambezi river. Because the basket designs repeat over relatively small intervals and are easily charted, they are ideal for stranded two-color knitting.

The *Nigeria* pullover is based on a fabric that comprises 4" (10-cm) woven bands that are sewn together, a common technique among the northern Yorubas of Nigeria. The pattern is made up of solid-colored stripes adjacent to patterned stripes in a combination that is both exciting and calming to knit. The sweater is worked sideways, from sleeve to sleeve, so that the stripes appear lengthwise on the garment, as in the original fabric.

DOUBLE KNITTING

While visiting Africa, I enjoyed a canoe trip down the Zambezi river, where I came very close to the wildlife—at times closer than was comfortable. On the other hand, this corner of the world is its own paradise. From the quiet of the canoe, sounds are filtered through the stillness, and all types of animals and birds can be sighted through the tall grasses and along the river's muddy banks.

The vests named for the magnificent *Giraffe* and *Zebra* showcase the animals' distinctive markings in knitted fabrics. The big, bold designs are best represented with double knitting, a technique that produces a firm, double-faced fabric. The technique is slow-going because it involves knitting one stitch for the right side followed by one stitch for the wrong side, but if the edges and seams are worked with care, the garment is reversible.

I invite you to pick up your needles and experience a little piece of this magnificent continent.

MARIANNE ISAGER
ÅRHUS, DENMARK

KUBA

Squares, diamonds, and striking contrasts between light and dark are prominent features in many African textiles. The yoke patterns on both versions of this pullover mimic the rotating motifs in a traditional woven fabric. In both versions, the lower body is worked in the round in mitered garter-stitch panels. The panel arrangement dictates the overall body size and shape of the zigzag at the base of the yoke. Entrelac squares, worked in either two-tone garter stitch or stripes of garter and stockinette stitch, are built one upon the other for the patterned yoke. On both versions, the V shape of the yoke is filled in with garter stitch that ends in a stand-up collar. The zippered version is finished off with a contrasting facing.

MATERIALS

SIZES 42 (46)" (106.5 [117] cm) finished chest/bust circumference. Shown in size 42" (106.5 cm) in black MC with two-tone squares and in size 46" (117 cm) in sage blue MC with striped squares.

YARN About 250 (325) g main color (MC) and 50 (100) g each of three contrasting colors (CC1, CC2, CC3) of fingering-weight (CYCA Super Fine #1) yarn.

Shown here:

For size 42": Isager Tvinni (100% merino lambswool; 558 yd [510 m]/100 g): #30 black (MC), 3 (4) skeins; #33 rust (CC1), #47 dark blue-gray (CC2), and #8s brown heather (CC3), 1 skein each.

For size 46": Isager Highland (100% pure new wool; 612 yd [560 m]/100 g): #10 sage blue (MC), 3, (4) skeins; #4 damask (rose heather; CC1) and #11 almond (greenish off-white heather; CC3), 1 (1) skein each. Isager Tvinni (100% merino lambswool; 558 yd [510 m]/100 g): #47 dark blue-gray (CC2), 1 skein.

NEEDLES U.S. size 2 (3 mm): 24" (60 cm) and 32" (80 cm) circular (cir), and set of double-pointed needles (dpn). Adjust needle size if necessary to obtain the correct gauge.

NOTIONS Stitch markers (m); removable markers or safety pins; stitch holders; 9" (23 cm) zipper for neck (optional); sharp-pointed sewing needle and matching thread for attaching zipper (optional); tapestry needle.

GAUGE 26 sts and 52 rows = 4" (10 cm) in garter st; 19 (20) sts and 38 (40) rows of two-tone garter st yoke square measure about 2¾ (3)" (7 [7.5] cm) square; 19 (20) sts and 34 (40) rows of striped yoke square measure about 2¾ (3)" (7 [7.5] cm) square.

STITCH GUIDE

TWO-TONE GARTER STITCH SQUARE

Note: These directions are for the basic square; instructions for how to join squares are given in the yoke directions.

Row 1: (RS) With first color given in directions or shown on diagram, knit or pick up and knit 19 (20) sts.

Row 2 and all even-numbered rows: (WS) Knit all sts with their same color.

Row 3: K1 with second color, twist yarns at color change to avoid leaving a hole, k18 (19) with first color.

Row 5: K2 with second color, twist yarns at color change to avoid leaving a hole, k17 (18) with first color.

Row 7: K3 with second color, twist yarns at color change to avoid leaving a hole, k16 (17) with first color.

Row 9 and all even-numbered rows through Row 37 (39): Cont in this manner, working 1 more st with second color every RS row; on last RS row there will be 18 (19) sts worked in second color and 1 st worked in first color.

Row 38 (40): Knit all sts with their same color.

STRIPED SQUARE

Note: These directions are for the basic square; instructions for how to join squares are given in the yoke directions.

Row 1: (RS) With CC2, knit or pick up and knit 19 (20) sts.

Rows 2–4: With CC2, knit.

Row 5: With CC3, knit.

Row 6: With CC3, purl.

Rep Rows 1–6 four (five) more times, then work Rows 1–4 once more—34 (40) rows completed; 6 (7) garter st stripes in CC2, 5 (6) St st stripes in CC3.

NOTES

• The schematic on page 12 has the details of the mitered panels and yoke squares sketched in for size 42". Overall garment measurements are given for both sizes on the schematic, but the placement of the miters and arrangement of the squares is slightly different for size 46".

- Work body and yoke according to separate instructions given for your size. Combined directions for the collar, sleeves, and finishing for both sizes begin on page 21.
- The mitered garter-stitch texture of the lower body and collar is created by working paired increases or decreases on either side of marked "peak" and "valley" stitches in order to make the garter-stitch ridges run in zigzag lines. Move the markers for these stitches up as you work.
- Read about entrelac knitting on page 24. The front and back yokes are identical and worked according to the diagrams for your size and chosen type of yoke square. For all diagrams, the squares are numbered in the order they are worked; arrows indicate the direction of knitting.
- On the yoke diagrams for two-tone squares, the unshaded triangles are worked with the lighter contrast color (CC3), and the shaded triangles are worked with the darker contrast color (CC2). On the yoke diagrams with striped squares, hatch marks indicate the orientation of the stripes.
- The yoke squares build one upon the other, entrelac-fashion, usually with stitches picked up along the edges of completed blocks and joined to live stitches of adjacent squares as described in the instructions. You may find it easier to work the individual squares with double-pointed needles.
- You may find it helpful to weave in the ends as you go, rather than have a large number of ends to weave in when finishing.

SIZE 42
BODY
Side triangle: (make 2)
With MC, CO 3 sts and work as foll:
Row 1: (WS) K3.
Row 2: (RS) K1, M1 (see Glossary, page 140), k1, M1, k1—5 sts.
Row 3: K5.
Row 4: [K1, M1] 4 times, k1—9 sts. Mark center st with removable marker or safety pin.
Row 5: K9.
Row 6: K1, M1, knit to marked center st, M1, k1 (center st), M1, knit to last st, M1, k1—4 sts inc'd.
Row 7: Knit.
Rep Rows 6 and 7 six more times—37 sts. Cut yarn and place sts on holder. Make a second triangle the same as the first.

Center front and back triangles: (make 4) With MC, CO 3 sts. Work Rows 1–7 as for side triangle—13 sts. Rep Rows 6 and 7 sixteen more times—77 sts. Cut yarn and place sts on holder. Make 3 more triangles the same way.

Join triangles: With RS facing, slip (sl) all 6 triangles to longer cir needle in the foll order: *One 37-st triangle, two 77-st triangles; rep from * once more—382 sts total. Slip sts around cir needle so that first st of rnd is the marked center st of a 37-st triangle, join MC. *Joining rnd:* K1 (center "peak" st of triangle), M1, k16, ssk (see Glossary, page 140), use backward loop method (see Glossary, page 139) to CO 1 st between triangles and mark this st as a

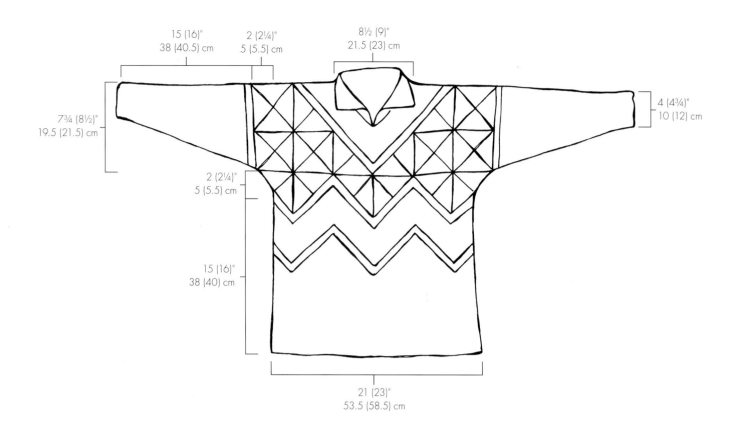

"valley" st, *k2tog, k36, M1, k1 (peak st), M1, k36, ssk, use backward loop method to CO 1 st between triangles and mark this st as a valley st;* rep from * to * once more for adjacent 77-st triangle, k2tog, k16, M1, k1 (peak st), M1, k16, ssk, CO 1 st between triangles and mark this st as a valley st; rep from * to * twice over next two 77-st triangles, k2tog, k16, M1, place marker (pm) on needle to indicate end of rnd—388 sts: 6 peak sts, 6 valley sts, 4 sections each in middle of both front and back with 38 sts between peaks and valleys, 1 section at each side of both front and back with 18 sts between peaks and valleys. Marked peak sts in the middle of the adjacent 18-st sections are the side "seams" of the lower body; rnd begins at left side. Purl 1 rnd across all sts.

Lower body: Cont in mitered garter st as foll:

Rnd 1: *K1 (peak st), M1, knit to 2 sts before next valley st, ssk, k1 (valley st), k2tog, knit to next peak st, M1; rep from * 5 more times.

Rnd 2: Purl.

Rep Rnds 1 and 2 until piece measures 10" (25.5 cm) from lower edge, measured straight up along peak st column at beg of rnd. If desired, change to CC1 and work in patt for 8 rnds (4 garter ridges) for optional accent stripe as shown in photo on page 8. Change to MC, or simply cont in MC if omitting the stripe, and work in patt until piece measures 14¼" (36 cm) from lower edge, measured

straight along peak st column at beg of rnd. Change to CC1 and work 7 rnds in patt. *Next rnd:* With CC1, *P2tog (peak st tog with next st), p56, p2tog (peak st tog with next st), p37, p2tog (valley st at center front tog with next st), p37, p2tog (peak st tog with next st), p56; rep from * once more—380 sts rem; piece measures about 15" (38 cm) from lower edge, measured straight up along peak st column at beg of rnd (side seam). Remove peak and valley markers. Place new markers on needle as foll to indicate groups of sts to be worked for yoke squares: Pm after the 190th st of rnd to divide sts in half for front and back; pm in center of front and back—95 sts on each side of center m. Count out groups of 19 sts on each side of center marker and pm after each group—front and back are each divided into 10 sections of 19 sts each.

FRONT YOKE

Refer to diagrams on page 14 to determine sequence, color placement, and direction of knitting for your choice of yoke squares, either two-tone garter st square or striped square (see Stitch Guide, page 10). *Note:* Because the smaller-size striped square has only 34 rows, it has only 17 rows available for joining to an adjacent 19-st group. To adjust for this, on 2 of the joining rows work either k3tog or sssk (see Glossary, page 140) in order to join 1 square st to 2 sts from the group being joined, and try to space these adjustment joining rows evenly.

Square 1: With RS facing, sl last 19 sts of front from cir to dpn. Join CC3 for two-tone square or CC2 for striped square and work Row 1 across these 19 sts. With RS still facing, sl next-to-last group of 19 sts of front to empty dpn. Turn and work Row 2 of square to last st of first group, ssk (last st of square on dpn tog with 1 st from next group on cir)—19 square sts on main dpn; 1 st joined from next group on cir needle. Cont in patt for square, joining other colors as needed, and *at the same time* work the last square st of every WS row tog with 1 st from next group of sts using ssk. When square has been completed, all sts of second group have been joined. Place 19 square sts on holder.

Square 2: With RS facing, sl 19 sts just after center marker from cir needle to dpn. Join CC3 for two-tone square or CC2 for striped square and work Row 1 across these 19 sts. With RS still facing, sl group of 19 sts on right side of center front to empty dpn. Turn and work Row 2 of square to last st of first group, ssk (last st of square tog with 1 st from second group)—19 square sts on main dpn; 1 st joined from second group. Cont in patt, joining the last square st of every WS row to 1 st on dpn for second group using ssk. Place 19 square sts on holder.

Square 3: With RS facing, sl second group of 19 sts of front from cir needle to dpn. Join CC3 for two-tone square or CC2 for striped square and work Row 1 across these 19 sts. With RS still facing, sl first 19 sts of front to empty dpn. Turn and work Row 2 of square to last st of first group, ssk (last st of square on dpn tog with 1 st from next group)—19 square sts on main dpn; 1 st joined from next group. Cont in patt, joining the last square st of every WS row to 1 st from next group using ssk. Leave sts on dpn.

Square 4: With CC3 for two-tone square or CC2 for striped square, CO 19 sts onto empty dpn. Work Row 1 of square to last st of first group, k2tog (last st of square tog with 1 st on needle from Square 3). Turn and work Row 2 of square to end. Cont in patt, joining the last square st of every RS row to 1 st from Square 3 using k2tog. Place 19 square sts on holder.

Square 5: With CC2 for both types of squares and RS facing, pick up and knit 18 sts along selvedge of Square 3. With RS still facing, sl next 19 sts of front from cir needle to empty dpn. At end of square needle, pick up a loop from selvedge of Square 3 and place it on the needle with sts from front, k2tog (picked-up loop tog with 1 st from next group)—19 square sts on main dpn; 1 st joined from next group; pick-up row counts as Row 1 of square. Cont in patt, joining the last square st of every RS row tog with 1 st from front using k2tog. Place 19 square sts on holder.

Square 6: Sl next group of 19 front sts from cir needle to dpn. With RS facing, join CC3 for two-tone square or CC2 for striped square. With RS still facing, return held sts of Square 2 to dpn. Work Row 1 of square to last st of first group, k2tog (last st of square tog with 1 st on needle from Square 2). Turn and work Row 2 of square to end. Cont in patt joining the last square st of every RS row tog with 1 st from Square 2 using k2tog. Place 19 square sts on holder.

Square 7: With CC2 for both types of squares and RS facing, pick up and knit 18 sts along selvedge of Square 2. With RS still facing, sl next 19 sts of front from cir needle to empty dpn. At end of square needle, pick up a loop from selvedge of Square 2 and place it on the needle with sts from front, k2tog (picked-up loop tog with 1 st from next group)—19 square sts on main dpn; 1 st joined from next group; pick-up row counts as Row 1 of square. Cont in patt, joining last square st of every RS row tog with 1 st from front using k2tog. Place 19 square sts on holder.

Square 8: Sl next group of 19 front sts from cir needle to dpn. With RS facing, join CC3 for two-tone square or CC2 for striped square. With RS still facing, return held sts of Square 1 to dpn. Work Row 1 of square to last st of first group, k2tog (last st of square tog with 1 st on needle from Square 1). Turn and work Row 2 of square to end. Cont in patt, joining the last square st of every RS row tog with 1 st from Square 3 using k2tog. Place 19 square sts on holder.

Square 9: With CC2 for both types of squares and RS facing, pick up and knit 19 sts along selvedge of Square 1. Cont in patt for without joining any sts. Leave sts on dpn.

Square 10: (half-square) With CC2 for both types of squares, CO 1 st onto empty dpn—counts as Row 1 of square. For two-tone square, work this half-square entirely in CC2; for striped square join CC3 as needed. Turn, ssk (1 st of square tog with 1 st on needle from Square 9)—counts as Row 2 of square. Turn, M1, k1—2 square sts; counts as Row 3 of square. Cont in this manner, working

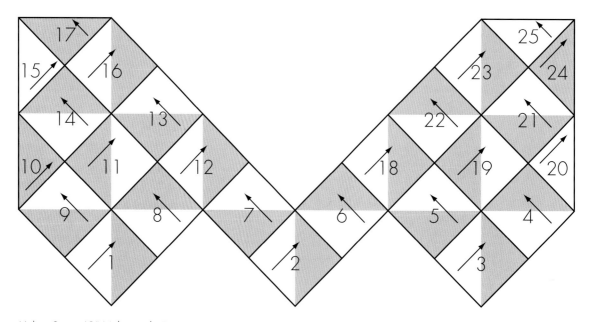

Kuba Size 42" Yoke with Two-Tone Squares

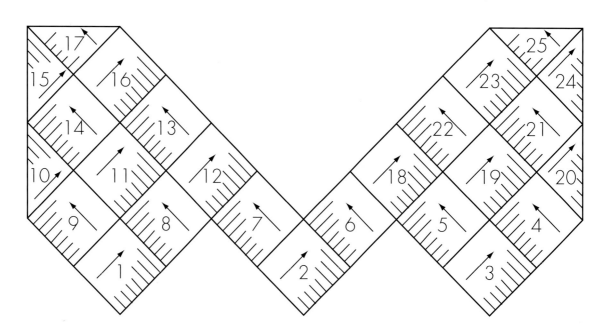

Kuba Size 42" Yoke with Striped Squares

the last st of every WS row tog with 1 st from Square 9, and inc 1 st before last st on every RS row—19 sts when square has been completed. *Note:* For striped square, you will also need to inc 1 st after the first st at beg of 2 evenly spaced WS rows to achieve the correct st count. Place 19 square sts on holder.

Square 11: With CC2 for both types of squares and RS facing, pick up and knit 19 sts along selvedge of Square 9—counts as Row 1 of square. With RS still facing, return held sts of Square 8 to dpn. Work Row 2 of square to last st of picked-up sts, ssk (last st of square tog with 1 st on needle from Square 8). Cont in patt, joining the last square st of every WS row tog with 1 st from Square 8 using ssk. Place 19 square sts on holder.

Square 12: With CC3 for two-tone square or CC2 for striped square and RS facing, pick up and knit 19 sts along selvedge of Square 8—counts as Row 1 of square. With RS still facing, return held sts of Square 7 to dpn. Work Row 2 of square to last st of picked-up sts, ssk (last st of square tog with 1 st on needle from Square 7). Cont in patt, joining the last square st of every WS row tog with 1 st from Square 7 using ssk. Place 19 square sts on holder.

Square 13: With CC2 for both types of squares and RS facing, pick up and knit 18 sts along selvedge of Square 12. With RS still facing, return held sts of Square 11 to dpn. At end of square needle, pick up a loop from selvedge of Square 12 and place it on the needle with sts from Square 11, k2tog (picked-up loop tog with 1 st from Square 11)—19 square sts on main dpn; 1 st joined from Square 11; pick-up row counts as Row 1 of square. Cont in patt, joining last square st of every RS row tog with 1 st from Square 11 using k2tog. Place 19 square sts on holder.

Square 14: With CC3 for two-tone square or CC2 for striped square and RS facing, pick up and knit 18 sts along selvedge of Square 11. With RS still facing, return held sts of Square 10 to dpn. At end of square needle, pick up a loop from selvedge of Square 11 and place it on the needle with sts from Square 10, k2tog (picked-up loop tog with 1 st from Square 10)—19 square sts on main dpn; 1 st joined from Square 10; pick-up row counts as Row 1 of square. Cont in patt, joining last square st of every RS row tog with 1 st from Square 10 using k2tog. Leave sts on dpn.

Square 15: (half-square) With CC3 for two-tone square or CC2 for striped square, CO 1 st—counts as Row 1 of square. For two-tone square, work this half-square entirely in CC3; for striped square join CC3 as needed. Turn, ssk (1 st of square tog with 1 st on needle from Square 14)—counts as Row 2 of square. Turn, M1, k1—2 square sts; counts as Row 3 of square. Cont in this manner, working the last st of every WS row tog with 1 st from Square 14 using ssk, and inc 1 st before last st on every RS row—19 sts when square has been completed. *Note:* For striped square, you will also need to inc 1 st after the first st at beg of 2 evenly spaced WS rows to achieve the correct st count. Place 19 square sts on holder.

Square 16: With CC3 for two-tone square or CC2 for striped square and RS facing, pick up and knit 19 sts along selvedge of Square 14—counts as Row 1 of square. With RS still facing, return held sts of Square 13 to dpn. Work Row 2 of square to last st of picked-up sts, ssk (last st of square tog with 1 st on needle from Square 13). Cont in patt, joining last square st of every WS row tog with 1 st from Square 13 using ssk. Place 19 square sts on holder.

Square 17: (half-square) With CC2 for both types of squares and RS facing, pick up and knit 18 sts along selvedge of Square 16. With RS still facing, return held sts of Square 15 to dpn. At end of square needle, pick up a loop from selvedge of Square 16 and place it on the needle with sts from Square 15, k2tog (picked-up loop tog with 1 st from Square 15)—19 square sts on main dpn; 1 st joined from next group; pick-up row counts as Row 1 of square. For two-tone square, work half-square entirely in CC2; for striped square, join CC3 as needed. Turn and work Row 2 of square to last 2 sts, ssk—18 sts. Cont in patt, joining last square st of every RS row tog with 1 st from Square 15 using k2tog, and working last 2 sts of every WS row as ssk. *Note:* For striped square, you will also need to work k2tog at beg of 2 evenly spaced RS rows. When 1 st rem, cut yarn and fasten off last st.

Square 18: With CC3 for two-tone square or CC2 for striped square and RS facing, pick up and knit 19 sts along selvedge of Square 6—counts as Row 1 of square. With RS still facing, return held sts of Square 5 to dpn. Work Row 2 of square to last st of picked-up sts, ssk (last st of square tog with 1 st on needle from Square 5). Cont in patt, joining the last square st of every WS row tog with 1 st from Square 5 using ssk. Place 19 square sts on holder.

Square 19: With CC2 for both types of squares and RS facing, pick up and knit 19 sts along selvedge of Square 5—counts as Row 1 of square. With RS still facing, return held sts of Square 4 to dpn. Work Row 2 of square to last st of picked-up sts, ssk (last st of square tog with 1 st on needle from Square 4). Cont in patt, joining last square st of every WS row tog with 1 st from Square 4 using ssk. Place 19 square sts on holder.

Square 20: (half-square) With CC3 for two-tone square or CC2 for striped square and RS facing, pick up and knit 19 sts along selvedge of Square 4—counts as Row 1 of square. For two-tone square, work this half-square entirely in CC3; for striped square, join CC3 as

needed. Work Row 2 of square to last 2 sts, ssk—18 sts. Cont in patt without joining any sts, and working the last 2 sts of every WS row as ssk. *Note:* For striped square, you will also need to work k2tog at beg of 2 evenly spaced RS rows. When 1 st rem, cut yarn and fasten off last st.

Square 21: With CC2 for both types of squares and RS facing, pick up and knit 18 sts along selvedge of Square 20. With RS still facing, return held sts of Square 19 to dpn. At end of square needle, pick up a loop from selvedge of Square 20 and place it on the needle with sts from Square 19, k2tog (picked-up loop tog with 1 st from Square 19)—19 square sts on main dpn; 1 st joined from Square 19; pick-up row counts as Row 1 of square. Cont in patt, joining last square st of every RS row tog with 1 st from Square 19 using k2tog. Place 19 square sts on holder.

Square 22: With CC3 for two-tone square or CC2 for striped square and RS facing, pick up and knit 18 sts along selvedge of Square 19. With RS still facing, return held sts of Square 18 to dpn. At end of square needle, pick up a loop from selvedge of Square 19 and place it on the needle with sts from Square 18, k2tog (picked-up loop tog with 1 st from Square 18)—19 square sts on main dpn; 1 st joined from Square 18; pick-up row counts as Row 1 of square. Cont in patt, joining last square st of every RS row tog with 1 st from Square 18 using k2tog. Place 19 square sts on holder.

Square 23: With CC3 for two-tone square or CC2 for striped square and RS facing, pick up and knit 19 sts along selvedge of Square 22—counts as Row 1 of square. With RS still facing, return held sts of Square 21 to dpn. Work Row 2 of square to last st of picked-up sts, ssk (last st of square tog with 1 st on needle from Square 21). Cont in patt, joining last square st of every WS row tog with 1 st from Square 21 using ssk. Place 19 square sts on holder.

Square 24: (half-square) With CC2 for both types of squares and RS facing, pick up and knit 19 sts along selvedge of Square 21—counts as Row 1 of square. For two-tone square, work half-square entirely in CC3; for striped square, join CC3 as needed. Work Row 2 of square to last 2 sts, ssk—18 sts. Cont in patt, working last 2 sts of every WS row as ssk. *Note:* For striped square, you will also need to work k2tog at beg of 2 evenly spaced RS rows. When 1 st rem, cut yarn and fasten off last st.

Square 25: (half-square) With CC3 for two-tone square or CC2 for striped square and RS facing, pick up and knit 18 sts along selvedge of Square 24. With RS still facing, return held sts of Square 23 to dpn. At end of square needle, pick up a loop from selvedge of Square 24 and place it on the needle with sts from Square 23, k2tog (picked-up loop tog with 1 st from Square 23)—19 square sts on main dpn; 1 st joined from Square 23; pick-up row counts as Row 1 of square. For two-tone square, work half-square entirely in CC3; for striped square, join CC3 as needed. Turn and work Row 2 of square to last 2 sts, ssk—18 sts. Cont in patt, joining last square st of every RS row tog with 1 st from Square 23 using k2tog, and working last 2 sts of every WS row as ssk. *Note:* For striped square, you will also need to work k2tog at beg of 2 evenly spaced RS rows. When 1 st rem, cut yarn and fasten off last st.

BACK YOKE

Work as for front yoke. Skip to directions for both sizes on page 21.

SIZE 46
BODY

Basic triangle: (make 8)

With MC, CO 3 sts and work as foll:

Row 1: (WS) K3.

Row 2: (RS) K1, M1 (see Glossary, page 140), k1, M1, k1—5 sts.

Row 3: K5.

Row 4: [K1, M1] 4 times, k1—9 sts. Mark center st with removable marker or safety pin.

Row 5: K9.

Row 6: K1, M1, knit to marked center st, M1, k1 (center st), M1, knit to last st, M1, k1—4 sts inc'd.

Row 7: Knit.

Rep Rows 6 and 7 seven more times—41 sts. Cut yarn and place sts on holder. Make 7 more triangles in the same manner.

Center front and back extensions: With RS facing, slip (sl) four 41-st triangles to longer cir needle—164 sts. *Set-up row:* K1 (edge st), M1, k19, M1, k1 (center "peak" st of triangle), M1, k18, ssk (see Glossary, page 140), use backward loop method (see Glossary, page 139) to CO 1 st between triangles and mark this st as a "valley" st, *k2tog, k18, M1, k1 (peak st), M1, k18, ssk, use backward loop method to CO 1 st between triangles and mark this st as a valley st;* rep from * to * once more, k2tog, k18, M1,

k1 (peak st), M1, k19, M1, k1 (edge st)—171 sts: 4 peak sts, 3 valley sts, 2 edge sts, 6 center sections with 20 sts each between peaks and valleys, 2 end sections with 21 sts each between peaks and edge sts. Knit 1 WS row.

Row 1: (RS) K1 (edge st), M1, *knit to next peak st, M1, k1 (peak st), M1, knit to 2 sts before next valley st, ssk, k1 (valley st), k2tog; rep from * 2 more times, knit to next peak st, M1, k1 (peak st), M1, knit to last st, M1, k1 (edge st)—4 sts inc'd; 2 sts inc'd in each end section.

Row 2: Knit.

Rep Rows 1 and 2 eight more times—207 sts: 4 peak sts, 3 valley sts, 2 edge sts, 6 center sections with 20 sts each between peaks and valleys, 2 end sections with 39 sts each between peaks and edge sts. Cut yarn and place sts on holder. With RS facing, slip (sl) rem four 41-st triangles to longer cir needle and work in the same manner—207 sts. Do not cut yarn.

Join triangles: With RS facing, sl 207 held sts to needle—414 sts total. Sl sts around cir needle so that first st of rnd is the valley st in the center of the six 20-st sections of one piece. Join MC. *Joining rnd:* *K1 (valley st), k2tog, knit to next peak st, M1, k1 (peak st), M1, knit to 2 sts before next valley st, ssk, k1 (valley st), k2tog, knit to next peak st, M1, k1 (peak st), M1, knit to 2 sts before edge st, ssk, k2tog (2 edge sts of adjacent pieces) and mark the resulting st as a new valley st, k2tog, knit to next peak st, M1, k1 (peak st), M1, knit to 2 sts before next valley st, ssk, k1 (valley st), k2tog, knit to next peak st, M1, k1 (peak st), M1, knit to 2 sts before next valley st, ssk; rep from * once more, place marker (pm) to indicate end of rnd—412 sts; the marked valley sts in center of each group of narrow panels are the side "seams" of the lower body; the valley sts between two adjacent 40-st sections are the centers of the front or back; rnd begins at left side in the center of six 20-st sections. Purl 1 rnd across all sts.

Lower body: Cont in mitered garter st as foll:

Rnd 1: *K1 (valley st), k2tog, knit to next peak st, M1, k1 (peak st), M1, knit to 2 sts before next valley st, ssk; rep from * 7 more times.

Rnd 2: Purl.

Rep these 2 rnds until piece measures 11" (28 cm) from lower edge, measured straight up along valley st column at beg of rnd. If desired, change to CC1 and work in patt for 8 rnds (4 garter ridges) for optional accent stripe as shown. Change to MC, or simply cont in MC if omitting the stripe, and work in patt until piece measures 15¼"

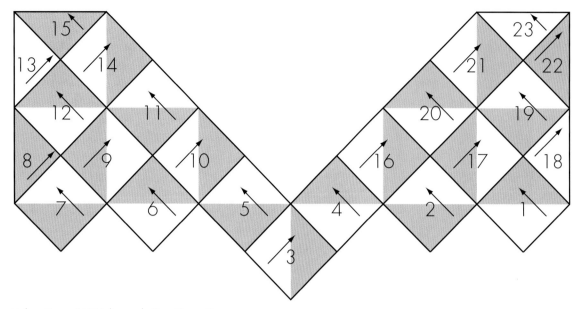

Kuba Size 46" Yoke with Two-Tone Squares

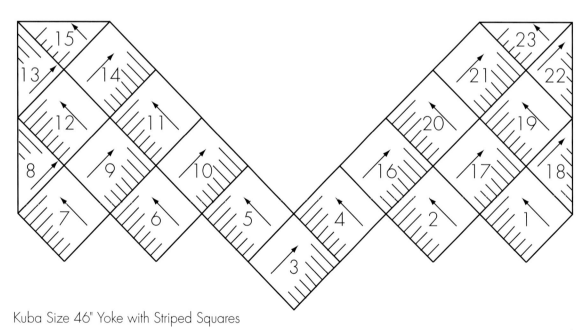

Kuba Size 46" Yoke with Striped Squares

(38.5 cm) from lower edge, measured straight along valley st column at beg of rnd. Change to CC1 and work 7 rnds in patt. *Next rnd:* With CC1, purl to peak st, *p2tog (peak st tog with next st), purl to next valley st, p2tog (valley st tog with next st), purl to next peak st, p2tog, purl past the next valley st without decreasing to foll peak st; rep from * 3 more times, ending last rep at end of rnd—400 sts; piece measures about 16" (40.5 cm) from lower edge, measured straight up along peak st column at beg of rnd (side seam). Remove peak and valley markers. Place new markers on needle as foll to indicate groups of sts to be worked for yoke squares: Pm after the 200th st of rnd to divide sts in half for front and back; pm in center of front and back—100 sts on each side of center m. Count out groups of 20 sts on each side of center marker and pm after each group—front and back are each divided into 10 sections of 20 sts each.

FRONT YOKE

Refer to diagrams on page 18 to determine sequence, color placement, and direction of knitting for your choice of yoke squares, either, two-tone garter st square or striped square (see Stitch Guide, page 10).

Square 1: With RS facing, sl first group of 20 sts of front from cir needle to dpn. With CC3 for two-tone square of CC2 for striped square and dpn, CO 20 sts onto same needle—first 20 sts to be worked with RS facing should be new CO sts. Work Row 1 of square to last st of CO sts, k2tog (last st of square tog with 1 st of next group), turn, work Row 2 of square to end. Cont in patt, joining the last square st of every RS row tog with 1 st from next group using k2tog. Place 20 square sts on holder.

Square 2: With RS facing, sl next 20 sts of front from cir needle to dpn. With RS still facing, sl foll 20 sts of front to another dpn. With RS facing, join CC2 for both types of squares to beg of first group of sts. Work Row 1 of square to last st of first group, k2tog (last st of square tog with 1 st of next group). Turn and work Row 2 of square to end. Cont in patt, joining the last square st of every RS row tog with 1 st from next group using k2tog. Place 20 square sts on holder.

Square 3: With RS facing, sl 20 sts before center front from cir needle to dpn. With RS still facing, sl 20 sts after center front from cir needle to another dpn. With RS facing, join CC3 for two-tone square or CC2 for striped square to beg of second group of sts (the ones after the center). Work

Row 1 of square. Turn and work Row 2 of square to last st of group, ssk (last st of square tog with 1 st of next group)—20 square sts on main dpn; 1 st joined from next group. Cont in patt, joining the last square st of every WS row to 1 st on dpn for second group using ssk. Leave sts on needle.

Square 4: With RS facing, sl 20 front sts between Square 2 and Square 3 from cir needle to dpn. With RS facing, join CC3 for two-tone square or CC2 for striped square. Work Row 1 of square to last st of first group, k2tog (last st of square tog with 1 st of Square 3). Turn and work Row 2 of square to end. Cont in patt, joining the last square st of every RS row tog with 1 st from Square 3 using k2tog. Place 20 square sts on holder.

Square 5: With CC2 for both types of squares and RS facing, pick up and knit 19 sts along selvedge of Square 3. With RS still facing, sl next 20 front sts from cir needle to empty dpn. At end of square needle, pick up a loop from selvedge of Square 3 and place it on the needle with sts from front, k2tog (picked-up loop tog with 1 st from next group)—20 square sts on main dpn; 1 st joined from next group; pick-up row counts as Row 1 of square. Cont in patt, joining last square st of every RS row tog with 1 st from front using k2tog. Place 20 square sts on holder.

Square 6: Sl next group of 20 front sts from cir needle to dpn. With RS facing, join CC3 for two-tone square or CC2 for striped square. With RS still facing, sl next 20 front sts to empty dpn. Work Row 1 of square to last st of first group, k2tog (last st of square tog with 1 st of next group). Turn and work Row 2 of square to end. Cont in patt, joining the last square st of every RS row tog with 1 st from next group using k2tog. Place 20 square sts on holder.

Square 7: With RS facing, sl last group of 20 sts of front from cir needle to dpn. With RS facing, join CC2 for both types of squares to beg of first group of sts. Cont in patt without joining any sts. Leave sts on dpn.

Square 8: (half-square) With CC2 for both types of squares, CO 1 st onto empty dpn—counts as Row 1 of square. For two-tone square, work this half-square entirely in CC2; for striped square, join CC3 as needed. Turn, ssk (1 st of square tog with 1 st on needle from Square 7)—counts as Row 2 of square. Turn, M1, k1—2 square sts; counts as Row 3 of square. Cont in this manner, working the last st of every WS row tog with 1 st from Square 7, and inc 1 st before last st on every RS row—20 sts when square has been completed. Place 20 square sts on holder.

Square 9: With CC2 for both types of squares and RS facing, pick up and knit 20 sts along selvedge of Square 7—counts as Row 1 of square. With RS still facing, return held sts of Square 6 to dpn. Work Row 2 of square to last st of picked-up sts, ssk (last st of square tog with 1 st on needle from Square 6). Cont in patt, joining the last square st of every WS row tog with 1 st from Square 6 using ssk. Place 20 square sts on holder.

Square 10: With CC3 for two-tone square or CC2 for striped square and RS facing, pick up and knit 20 sts along selvedge of Square 6—counts as Row 1 of square. With RS still facing, return held sts of Square 5 to dpn. Work Row 2 of square to last st of picked-up sts, ssk (last st of square tog with 1 st on needle from Square 5). Cont in patt, joining the last square st of every WS row tog with 1 st from Square 5 using ssk. Place 20 square sts on holder.

Square 11: With CC2 for both types of squares and RS facing, pick up and knit 19 sts along selvedge of Square 10. With RS still facing, return held sts of Square 9 to dpn. At end of square needle, pick up a loop from selvedge of Square 10 and place it on the needle with sts from Square 9, k2tog (picked-up loop tog with 1 st from Square 9)—20 square sts on main dpn; 1 st joined from Square 9; pick-up row counts as Row 1 of square. Cont in patt, joining last square st of every RS row tog with 1 st from Square 9 using k2tog. Place 20 square sts on holder.

Square 12: With CC3 for two-tone square and CC2 for striped square and RS facing, pick up and knit 19 sts along selvedge of Square 9. With RS still facing, return held sts of Square 8 to dpn. At end of square needle, pick up a loop from selvedge of Square 9 and place it on the needle with sts from Square 8, k2tog (picked-up loop tog with 1 st from Square 8)—20 square sts on main dpn; 1 st joined from Square 8; pick-up row counts as Row 1 of square. Cont in patt, joining last square st of every RS row tog with 1 st from Square 8 using k2tog. Leave sts on dpn.

Square 13: (half-square) With CC3 for two-tone square or CC2 for striped square, CO 1 st—counts as Row 1

of square. For two-tone square, work this half-square entirely in CC3; for striped square join CC3 as needed. Turn, ssk (1 st of square tog with 1 st on needle from Square 12)—counts as Row 2 of square. Turn, M1, k1—2 square sts; counts as Row 3 of square. Cont in this manner, working the last st of every WS row tog with 1 st from Square 12 using ssk, and inc 1 st before last st on every RS row—20 sts when square has been completed. Place 20 square sts on holder.

Square 14: With CC3 for two-tone square or CC2 for striped square and RS facing, pick up and knit 20 sts along selvedge of Square 12—counts as Row 1 of square. With RS still facing, return held sts of Square 11 to dpn. Work Row 2 of square to last st of picked-up sts, ssk (last st of square tog with 1 st on needle from Square 11). Cont in patt, joining last square st of every WS row tog with 1 st from Square 11 using ssk. Place 20 square sts on holder.

Square 15: (half-square) With CC2 for both types of squares and RS facing, pick up and knit 19 sts along selvedge of Square 14. With RS still facing, return held sts of Square 13 to dpn. At end of square needle, pick up a loop from selvedge of Square 14 and place it on the needle with sts from Square 13, k2tog (picked-up loop tog with 1 st from Square 13)—20 square sts on main dpn; 1 st joined from Square 13; pick-up row counts as Row 1 of square. For two-tone square, work half-square entirely in CC2; for striped square join CC3 as needed. Turn and work Row 2 of square to last 2 sts, ssk—19 sts. Cont in patt, joining last square st of every RS row tog with 1 st from Square 13 using k2tog, and working last 2 sts of every WS row as ssk. When 1 st rem, cut yarn and fasten off last st.

Square 16: With CC3 for two-tone square or CC2 for striped square and RS facing, pick up and knit 20 sts along selvedge of Square 4—counts as Row 1 of square. With RS still facing, return held sts of Square 2 to dpn. Work Row 2 of square to last st of picked-up sts, ssk (last st of square tog with 1 st on needle from Square 2). Cont in patt, joining the last square st of every WS row tog with 1 st from Square 2 using ssk. Place 20 square sts on holder.

Square 17: With CC2 for both types of squares and RS facing, pick up and knit 20 sts along selvedge of Square

2—counts as Row 1 of square. With RS still facing, return held sts of Square 1 to dpn. Work Row 2 of square to last st of picked-up sts, ssk (last st of square tog with 1 st on needle from Square 1). Cont in patt, joining last square st of every WS row tog with 1 st from Square 1 using ssk. Place 20 square sts on holder.

Square 18: (half-square) With CC3 for two-tone square or CC2 for striped square and RS facing, pick up and knit 20 sts along selvedge of Square 1—counts as Row 1 of square. For two-tone square, work this half-square entirely in CC3; for striped square, join CC3 as needed. Work Row 2 of square to last 2 sts, ssk—19 sts. Cont in patt without joining any sts, and working the last 2 sts of every WS row as ssk. When 1 st rem, cut yarn and fasten off last st.

Square 19: With CC2 for both types of squares and RS facing, pick up and knit 19 sts along selvedge of Square 18. With RS still facing, return held sts of Square 17 to dpn. At end of square needle, pick up a loop from selvedge of Square 18 and place it on the needle with sts from Square 17, k2tog (picked-up loop tog with 1 st from Square 17)—20 square sts on main dpn; 1 st joined from Square 17; pick-up row counts as Row 1 of square. Cont in patt, joining last square st of every RS row tog with 1 st from Square 17 using k2tog. Place 20 square sts on holder.

Square 20: With CC3 for two-tone square or CC2 for striped square and RS facing, pick up and knit 19 sts along selvedge of Square 17. With RS still facing, return held sts of Square 16 to dpn. At end of square needle, pick up a loop from selvedge of Square 17 and place it on the needle with sts from Square 16, k2tog (picked-up loop tog with 1 st from Square 16)—20 square sts on main dpn; 1 st joined from Square 16; pick-up row counts as Row 1 of square. Cont in patt, joining last square st of every RS row tog with 1 st from Square 16 using k2tog. Place 20 square sts on holder.

Square 21: With CC3 for two-tone square or CC2 for striped square and RS facing, pick up and knit 20 sts along selvedge of Square 20—counts as Row 1 of square. With RS still facing, return held sts of Square 19 to dpn. Work Row 2 of square to last st of picked-up sts, ssk (last st of square tog with 1 st on needle from Square 19).

Cont in patt, joining last square st of every WS row tog with 1 st from Square 19 using ssk. Place 20 square sts on holder.

Square 22: (half-square) With CC2 for both types of squares and RS facing, pick up and knit 20 sts along selvedge of Square 19—counts as Row 1 of square. For two-tone square, work this half-square entirely in CC3; for striped square, join CC3 as needed. Work Row 2 of square to last 2 sts, ssk—19 sts. Cont in patt, working last 2 sts of every WS row as ssk. When 1 st rem, cut yarn and fasten off last st.

Square 23: (half-square) With CC3 for two-tone square or CC2 for striped square and RS facing, pick up and knit 19 sts along selvedge of Square 22. With RS still facing, return held sts of Square 21 to dpn. At end of square needle, pick up a loop from selvedge of Square 22 and place it on the needle with sts from Square 21, k2tog (picked-up loop tog with 1 st from Square 21)—20 square sts on main dpn; 1 st joined from Square 21; pick-up row counts as Row 1 of square. For two-tone square, work this half-square entirely in CC3; for striped square, join CC3 as needed. Turn, and work Row 2 of square to last 2 sts, ssk—19 sts. Cont in patt, joining last square st of every RS row tog with 1 st from Square 21 using k2tog, and working last 2 sts of every WS row as ssk. When 1 st rem, cut yarn and fasten off last st.

BACK YOKE
Work as for front yoke.

BOTH SIZES
JOIN SHOULDERS
With CC2, RS facing, and shorter cir needle, pick up and knit 25 (27) sts evenly across half-square at top of left front shoulder. With other end of cir needle, pick up and knit 25 (27) sts evenly across half-square at top of left back shoulder. Turn work carefully inside out, and with right sides touching, use the three-needle bind-off technique (see Glossary, page 140) and spare dpn to join left shoulders tog. Rep for right shoulder.

NECK STRIPE
With shorter cir needle, MC, RS facing, and beg at left shoulder seam, *pick up and knit 1 st in shoulder seam and mark this st as a valley st, either k19 (20) held sts or

pick up and knit 19 (20) sts along selvedge of each of the 4 yoke squares to center, pick up and knit 1 st in center and mark this st as a valley st, either k19 (20) held sts or pick up and knit 19 (20) sts along selvedge of each of the 4 yoke squares to other shoulder; rep from * once more—308 (324) sts. Join for working in the rnd and pm to indicate beg of rnd. *Next rnd:* *P1 (valley st), p2tog, purl to 2 sts before next valley st, p2tog; rep from * 3 more times—300 (316) sts.

Rnd 1: *K1 (valley st), k2tog, knit to 2 sts before next valley st, ssk; rep from * 3 more times—8 sts dec'd.

Rnd 2: Purl.

Rep Rnds 1 and 2 two more times—276 (292) sts; 4 garter ridges in MC.

COLLAR

Choose foldover or zipper version.

FOLDOVER COLLAR

Change to CC1 for two-tone squares version or CC2 for striped squares version. Rep the last 2 rnds of neck stripe 18 (19) more times—132 (140) sts; 18 (19) garter ridges in CC. Break yarn. Change to MC. Sl the first 33 (35) sts

of rnd and rejoin MC with RS facing to center front valley st. Collar is worked back and forth in rows of mitered garter st as foll: *Set-up row:* (RS) K1 (now edge st, formerly valley st at center front), k2tog, k30 (32) to marked st at shoulder, M1, k1 (now peak st, formerly valley st at shoulder), M1, k30 (32) to marked st at center back, ssk, k1 (valley st), k2tog, k30 (32) to marked st at next shoulder, M1, k1 (now peak st, formerly valley st), M1, k32 (34) to end, and mark last st for edge st—133 (141) sts; 5 marked sts: 1 at each shoulder, 1 at center back, 1 at each side of front opening; 4 sections of 32 (34) sts each between the marked sts.

Row 1: (WS) Knit.

Row 2: (RS) K1 (edge st), k2tog, knit to peak st at shoulder, M1, k1 (peak st), M1, knit to 2 sts before valley st at center back, ssk, k1 (valley st), k2tog, knit to peak st at shoulder, M1, k1 (peak st), M1, knit 2 sts before edge st at end of row, ssk, k1.

Rep Rows 1 and 2 until piece measures 2½" (6.5 cm) from end of CC insert, measured straight along peak st column at shoulder, ending with a WS row. Fill in the valley of each mitered section of collar separately using short-rows as foll:

KNITTING OUT OF

Right front:

Row 1: (RS) K1 (marked st), k2tog, knit to 3 sts before next marked st, k2tog, k1, turn—2 sts dec'd.

Row 2: (WS) Knit across sts just worked.

Row 3: K1, k2tog, knit to 3 sts before turning point at end of section, k2tog, k1, turn—2 sts dec'd.

Rep Rows 2 and 3 until 4 sts rem. On the next row, k2tog twice—2 sts rem. On the foll row, k2tog, cut yarn, and draw through rem st.

Right back and left back: For right back, rejoin yarn with RS facing and work as for right front over next group of sts. Rep over foll group of sts for left back.

Left front: Left front section has 1 extra st because 1 extra was added at the left front edge when collar divided. Work as for right front until 5 sts rem. On the foll row, k2tog, k1, k2tog—3 sts rem. On the foll row, k3tog, cut yarn and draw through rem st.

ZIPPERED COLLAR

Break yarn. Sl sts on needle to valley st at center front. With RS facing, rejoin CC1 for two-tone squares version or CC2 for striped squares version to center front valley st—276 (292) sts; 4 marked sts: 1 at each shoulder and center front and back; 4 sections of 68 (72) sts between the marked sts. Next dec section of collar is worked back and forth in rows of mitered garter st as foll: *Set-up row:* (RS) K1 (now edge st, formerly valley st), k2tog, *knit to 2 sts before next valley st, ssk, k1 (valley st), k2tog; rep from * 2 more times, knit to end without decreasing, mark last st (edge st)—269 (285) sts rem; 5 marked sts: 1 at each shoulder, 1 at center back, 1 on each side of front opening; 4 sections of 66 (70) sts each between the marked sts.

Row 1: (WS) Knit.

Row 2: (RS) K1 (edge st), k2tog, *knit to 2 sts before next valley st, ssk, k1 (valley st), k2tog; rep from * 2 more times, knit to last 3 sts, k2tog, k1—8 sts dec'd.

Rep the last 2 rows 16 (17) more times, then work Row 1 once more—133 (141) sts rem; 18 (19) garter ridges in CC; 5 marked sts: 1 at each shoulder, 1 at center back, 2 on each side of front opening; 4 sections of 32 (34) sts each bet marked sts. Change to MC and complete as for foldover collar, beg from where foldover collar has 133 (141) sts, using CC3 for striped version.

COLLAR FACING (BOTH VERSIONS)

With CC1, shorter cir needle, and RS of garment facing, pick up and knit 96 (104) sts along now straight top edge of collar. Work St st back and forth in rows until facing measures 2½" (6.5 cm) from pick-up row, ending with a WS row. *Next row:* (RS) K24 (26), join second ball of yarn and BO center 48 (52) sts, work to end—24 (26) sts each side. On the foll WS row, p24 (26) across first section, CO 6 sts, work to end across second section. On the next RS row, k24 (26) across first section, CO 6 sts, work across all sts of second section—30 (32) sts at each side; 6 sts CO at shoulder seam for each side. Purl 1 row. *Dec row:* (RS) Working each side separately, for first section work to last 2 sts, k2tog; for second section, ssk, work to end—1 st dec'd at each side. Work 1 row even. Rep the shaping of the last 2 rows 23 (25) more times—6 sts rem at each side. Work even until facing reaches to top of yoke squares. BO rem sts.

SLEEVES

With shorter cir needle, CC1 for two-tone version or CC2 for striped version, RS facing, and beg at base of half-square at left front, pick up and knit 24 (26) sts along selvedge of each of the 4 half-squares at left armhole edge—96 (104) sts. Do not join. Knit 7 rows—8 garter ridges. Change to MC. *Dec row:* (RS) K1, k2tog, knit to last 3 sts, ssk, k1—2 sts dec'd. Knit 5 rows. Cont in garter st, rep the shaping of the last 6 rows 22 (21) more times—50 (60) sts rem. Work even in garter st until piece measures 15 (16)" (38 [40.5] cm) from pick-up row, or desired length. BO all sts. Work right sleeve in the same manner, picking up along 4 half-squares at right armhole.

FINISHING
ZIPPER

For zippered collar, align top of zipper with upper edge of collar and sew in place using sewing needle and thread (see Glossary, page 141). With yarn threaded on a tapestry needle, close any gap at center front below zipper if necessary. With sewing needle and thread, sew center front edges of collar facing to zipper tape so as to cover zipper tape with facing.

With yarn threaded on a tapestry needle, tack shaped lower edge of facing to inside of sweater as invisibly as possible. Sew sleeve and side seams. Weave in loose ends. Carefully steam-press on WS under a damp cloth.

The English word for entrelac comes from the French word *entrelacer,* which means to interlace. It is a method of knitting in which blocks, rather than rows, are worked one on top of, and adjacent to, one another. Entrelac begins with a base row, or tier, of triangles. The size of the base triangles determines the dimensions of the subsequent blocks. Stitches are picked up along the edges of the triangles and are worked into blocks that join adjacent triangles. The knitting grows in tiers of blocks that alternate directions and result in a patchwork look.

Variations of this technique are used for Kuba (page 8), Zaire (page 26), Congo (page 34), African Domino Cardigan (page 44), and African Domino Pullover (page 52). Details for the variations are given within the project instructions.

KNITTING ENTRELAC

To try out the technique, cast on 45 stitches. To simplify the instructions for the sample swatch, some stitches are placed on holders; this is not necessary with most projects.

FOUNDATION TIER

The foundation tier is made up of five garter-stitch half-blocks, or triangles. The triangles are worked from right to left as follows:

Triangle:

Row 1: K2, turn the work around.
Row 2: K2, turn.
Rows 3 and 4: K3, turn.
Rows 5 and 6: K4, turn.
Rows 7 and 8: K5, turn.
Rows 9 and 10: K6, turn.
Rows 11 and 12: K7, turn.
Rows 13 and 14: K8, turn.
Rows 15 and 16: K9, turn.
Row 17: K7, do not turn. This completes the first triangle, which remains on the right needle as the next triangle is worked.

Repeat Rows 1–17 until there are five groups of 9 stitches each. The triangle shapes are easiest to see if each group of stitches is placed on a separate needle. To facilitate the instructions for Tier 1, turn the work around so that the working yarn is at the right edge of the tier (Figure 1). This is now the right side (RS) of the work, and the last triangle completed is marked as Triangle 1.

TIER 1

The first tier consists of squares or rectangles worked at right angles to the foundation triangles. With RS facing, knit across the 9 stitches of Triangle 1 and place these stitches on a holder. Continue as follows:

Block 1: With a spare needle, pick up and knit 9 stitches along the selvedge edge of Triangle 1. Turn the work, then knit these 9 stitches again.

Row 1: (WS) K8, k2tog (last picked-up stitch with first live stitch of Triangle 2), turn the work around—1 triangle stitch has been decreased.

Row 2: (WS) K9.

Repeat Rows 1 and 2 until all the stitches from Triangle 1 have been used, ending with Row 1—9 stitches remain for Block 1. These stitches will not be worked again until Tier 2.

Block 2: Block 2 joins Triangles 2 and 3. With RS facing and using the needle containing 9 stitches of Block 1, pick up and knit 9 stitches along the selvedge edge of Triangle 2. Turn work. With wrong side facing, knit these 7 stitches. Continue as follows:

Row 1: (RS) K8, k2tog (last picked-up stitch tog with first live stitch of Triangle 3), turn the work around.

Row 2: (WS) K9.

Repeat Rows 1 and 2 until no triangle stitches remain—9 stitches remain for Block 2. These stitches will not be worked again until Tier 3.

Blocks 3 and 4: Work as for Block 2, picking up stitches along the selvedge edge of Triangles 3 and 4, respectively. This completes Tier 1 (Figure 2).

TIER 2

The second tier consists of squares or rectangles worked at right angles to the foundation triangles, and from left to right across the previous tier. In order to reverse the direction of work, the wrong side will be facing as stitches are picked up along the edges of the blocks. Therefore, these stitches are picked up and purled (see Glossary, page 141).

Block 5: With WS facing, knit across the 9 stitches of Block 4 and place these stitches on a holder.

With WS still facing, use a spare needle to pick up and purl 9 stitches along the selvedge edge of Block 4. Turn the work, then knit these 9 stitches. Continue as follows:

Row 1: (WS) K8, k2tog through the back loops, turn,

Row 2: K9.

Repeat Rows 1 and 2 until all the stitches of Block 3 have been worked ending with Row 1—9 stitches remain for Block 5.

Blocks 6 and 7: Work as for Block 5, picking up stitches along the selvedge edge of Blocks 3 and 2, respectively. This completes Tier 2 (Figure 3).

Subsequent tiers are worked in the same manner, each tier connecting live stitches and picked-up stitches of the blocks in the previous tier. For tiers that progress from right to left, the right side faces when stitches are picked up to begin each block. Therefore, the stitches are picked up and knitted. For tiers that progress from left to right, the wrong side faces so stitches are picked up and purled.

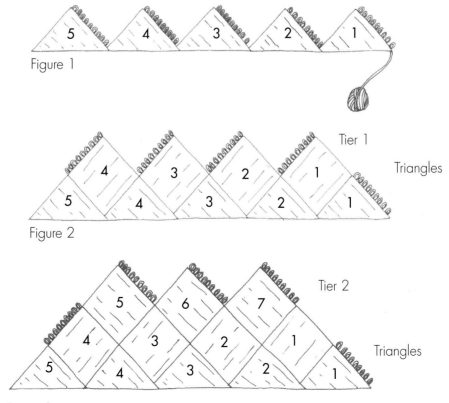

Figure 1

Figure 2

Tier 1

Triangles

Figure 3

Tier 2

Triangles

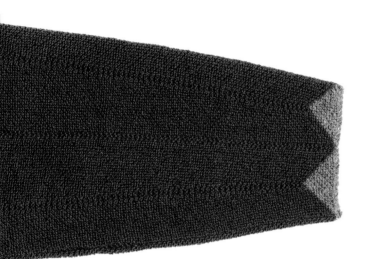

The geometric design for this sweater is based on a small detail in a woven cloth that originates from the western part of the Congo, formerly known as Zaire. The lower body is worked back and forth in rows in a series of mitered garter-stitch panels that encompass the entire body circumference; the selvedges create a slit that falls slightly to the back of the left side. The upper body is worked in four tiers of entrelac garter-stitch squares that are turned on their points to form diamonds. Each tier is framed with mitered garter- and stockinette-stitch stripes. The sleeves are worked outward from the upper body in mitered garter-stitch panels similar to those worked for the lower body; triangles of contrasting colors fill in the uneven edges at the cuffs. The front-split collar is also worked in mitered garter stitch, with color changes aligned with the miters.

MATERIALS

SIZES 40½ (43½, 46½)" (103 [110.5, 118] cm) finished chest/bust circumference. Shown in size 40½" (103 cm).

YARN About 200 (225, 250) g of main color (MC), 75 (100, 125) g each of three contrasting colors (CC1, CC2, CC3), and 25 g of accent color (A) of fingering-weight (CYCA Super Fine #1) yarn.

Shown here: Isager Tvinni (100% merino lambswool 558 yd [510 m]/100 g): #47 dark blue-gray (MC), 2 (3, 3) skeins; #30 black (CC1), #8s dark brown heather (CC2), and #7s light brown heather (CC3), 1 (1, 2) skein(s) each; #3 ochre yellow (A), 1 skein.

NEEDLES U.S. size 2 (3 mm): straight, 24" (60 cm) and 32" (80 cm) circular (cir), and optional set of 2 double-pointed (dpn) for working garter st squares. Adjust needle size if necessary to obtain the correct gauge.

NOTIONS Stitch markers (m); removable markers or safety pins; stitch holders; tapestry needle.

GAUGE 28 sts and 56 rows = 4" (10 cm) in garter st; 33 (36, 39) sts and 66 (72, 78) rows for garter st square measure about 4¾ (5⅛, 5½)" (12 [13, 14] cm) square.

STITCH GUIDE
GARTER STITCH SQUARE

Note: These directions are for the basic square; instructions for how to join squares are given in the directions.

First set-up row: (RS) Knit or CO 22 (24, 26) sts with CC2 or CC3 as given in directions, knit or CO 11 (12, 13) sts with CC1 (black in sweater shown), twisting yarns at color change to avoid leaving a hole—33 (36, 39) sts total.

Next 21 (23, 25) rows: Knit all sts with their same colors—22 (24, 26) rows and 11 (12, 13) garter ridges completed.

Second set-up row: (RS) K11 (12, 13) with CC2 or CC3 as established, join A (ochre yellow in sweater shown) for center of square, k11 (12, 13) with A, k11 (12, 13) with CC1.

Next 21 (23, 25) rows: Knit all sts with their same colors—44 (48, 52) rows and 22 (24, 26) garter ridges completed. Break off A.

Third set-up row: (RS) K11 (12, 13) with CC2 or CC3 as established, k22 (24, 26) with CC1.

Next 21 (23, 25) rows: Knit all sts with their same colors—66 (72, 78) rows and 33 (36, 39) garter ridges completed. Place sts on holder or scrap yarn.

NOTES

• The mitered garter stitch texture of the lower body, sleeves, and collar is created by working paired

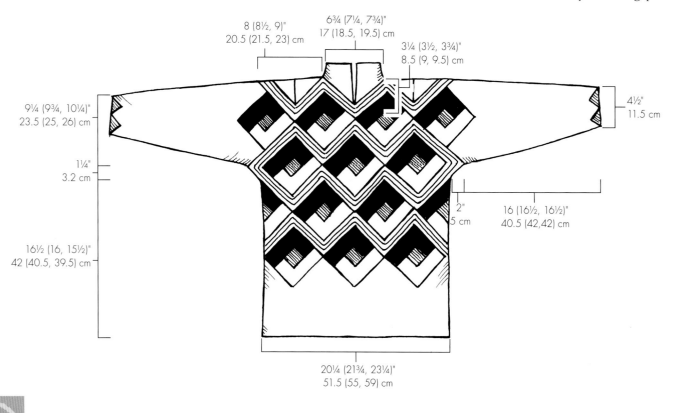

increases or decreases on either side of marked "peak" and "valley" stitches in order to make the garter stitch ridges run in zigzag lines. Move the markers for these stitches up as you work.

- The lower body is worked back and forth in rows in one piece, then joined into a round to the armholes. The piece divides again for working the front and back separately to the shoulders, and then is joined again for working the shoulder yoke in the round.

- Read about entrelac knitting on page 24. The tiers of entrelac squares begin with live stitches from sections of the lower body or mitered stripes and are joined to live stitches in adjacent sections as described in the instructions. You may find it easier to work the individual squares using a pair of double-pointed needles.

- The sweater shown measures 27" (68.5 cm) from shoulder to lower edge for all sizes. To customize the length, work more or fewer rows in mitered garter stitch with MC before beginning the first tier of garter stitch squares. Every 12 rows added or subtracted will increase or decrease the overall length by about 1" (2.5 cm).

- You may find it helpful to weave in the ends as you go, rather than have a large number of ends to weave in when finishing.

LOWER BODY
BOTTOM TRIANGLE (MAKE 6)
With MC and straight needles, CO 3 sts and work as foll:
Row 1: (WS) K3.
Row 2: (RS) K1, M1 (see Glossary, page 140), k1, M1, k1—5 sts.
Row 3: K5.
Row 4: [K1, M1] 4 times, k1—9 sts. Mark center st with removable marker or safety pin.
Row 5: K9.
Row 6: K1, M1, knit to marked center st, M1, k1 (center st), M1, knit to last st, M1, k1—4 sts inc'd.
Row 7: Knit.
Rep Rows 6 and 7 thirteen (fourteen, sixteen) more times, inc 0 (1, 0) st on each side of center marked st on last WS row—65 (71, 77) sts. Cut yarn and place sts on holder. Make 5 more triangles the same as the first.

JOIN TRIANGLES
With RS facing, place all 6 triangles on longer cir needle—390 (426, 462) sts. Join MC.
Joining row: (RS) K1 and mark this st as an edge st, *knit

to marked center st of triangle, M1, k1 ("peak" st), M1, knit to last 2 sts of triangle, ssk (see Glossary, page 140), use backward loop method (see Glossary, page 139) to CO 1 st between triangles and mark this st as a "valley" st, k2tog (first 2 sts of next triangle); rep from * 4 more times, knit to marked center st of last triangle, M1, k1 (peak st), M1, knit to end and mark last st as an edge st—397 (433, 469) sts rem: 6 peak sts, 5 valley sts, 1 edge st at each side, 12 sections with 32 (35, 38) sts between marked sts. Knit 1 WS row. Cont in mitered garter st as foll:
Row 1: (RS) K1 (edge st), k2tog, *knit to peak st, M1, k1 (peak st), M1, knit to 2 sts before valley st, ssk, k1 (valley st), k2tog; rep from * 4 more times, knit to last peak st, M1, k1 (peak st), M1, knit to last 3 sts, ssk, k1 (edge st).
Row 2: Knit.
Rep these 2 rows until piece measures about 5½ (4¼, 2¾)" (14 [11, 7] cm) from lower edge, measured straight up along selvedge or column of valley sts, and about 8½ (7½, 6½)" (21.5 [19, 16.5] cm), measured straight up along a column of peak sts, ending with a RS row (see Notes if customizing length). On the next WS row, knit to last st, slide sts along needle so first and last st are next to one another, knit these 2 sts tog to join into a rnd, mark this st as both a valley st and first st of the new rnd—396 (432, 468) sts rem: 6 peak sts, 6 valley sts, 12 sections with 32 (35, 38) sts between marked sts. Break MC. Turn work so RS is facing.

SQUARES TIER 1
Square 1: With RS facing, join CC2 to beg of new valley st at beg of rnd. Work first set-up row of garter st square (see Stitch Guide, page 28) over 33 (36, 39) sts, joining CC1 for last 11 (12, 13) sts. Turn. *Next row:* (WS) Work 32 (35, 38) sts for garter st square, ssk (last st of square tog with 1 st from end of rnd)—still 33 (36, 39) square sts on right-hand needle; 1 st joined from next section. Work next RS row of garter st square. Rep the last 2 rows until 66 (72, 78) rows of garter st square have been completed, joining the last st of garter st square to 1 st from next section using ssk at the end of every WS row. Break yarns. Place 33 (36, 39) garter st square sts on holder.

Square 2: With RS facing, sl the next 33 (36, 39) sts of rnd without working them. Join CC2 to next valley st. Work as for Square 1, joining last st on each WS row of square to 1 st of adjacent section using ssk. Place garter st square sts on holder.

Square 3: Work as for Square 2, using CC3.

Squares 4 and 5: Work as for Square 2, using CC2.

Square 6: Work as for Square 2, using CC3.
The point between Squares 1 and 2 should be aligned with the peak st of the first lower edge triangle, and correspond to the left side "seam" of the garment; the back slit for the lower body will be 3 to 4" (7.5 to 10 cm) in from this side "seam," aligned with the lower point of Square 1.

MITERED STRIPE 1

Place sts of all squares on longer cir needle with RS facing—198 (216, 234) sts; there will be gaps between the groups of sts. Join MC to beg of live Square 2 sts at side "seam."

Rnd 1: With MC, *k1 and mark this st as a valley st, k2tog, k30 (33, 36), pick up and knit 3 sts in corner of square and mark the center picked-up st as a peak st, pick up and knit 31 (34, 37) sts along selvedge of square; beg with the next group of live sts on needle, rep from * 5 more times—396 (432, 468) sts.

Rnd 2: With MC, knit.

Rnd 3: Change to CC3. *K1 (valley st), k2tog, knit to peak st, M1, k1 (peak st), M1, knit to 2 sts before valley st, ssk; rep from * 5 more times.

Rnd 4: With CC3, purl.

Rnd 5: Change to MC and rep Rnd 3.

Rnd 6: With MC, knit.

Rnds 7–14: Rep Rnds 3–6 two more times—7 two-rnd stripes completed: 4 St st stripes with MC, 3 garter st stripes with CC3. Break yarn.

SQUARES TIER 2

Square 1: With RS facing, join CC2 to valley st at beg of rnd. Work as for Square 1 in Tier 1.

Squares 2 and 3: Work as for Square 2 of Tier 1, using CC3.

Square 4: Work as for Square 2 of Tier 1, using CC2.

Squares 5 and 6: Work as for Square 2 of Tier 1, using CC3.
Piece measures about 16½ (16, 15½)" (42 [40.5, 39.5] cm) from beg, measured straight up along side "seam," which runs through the center of Square 1 of this tier.

UPPER FRONT

The work divides for back and front beg with this stripe.

MITERED STRIPE 2

Place sts of Squares 2, 3, and 4 of Tier 2 on longer cir needle with RS facing for front—99 (108, 117) sts total; there will be gaps between the groups of sts. Join MC to beg of selvedge of Square 1 of Tier 2, at top point of square. Using the knitted method (see Glossary, page 139), CO 12 sts onto left-hand needle.

Row 1: (RS) With MC, k12 new CO sts, pick up and knit 33 (36, 39) sts along selvedge of square, *k33 (36, 39) live sts and mark first st as a valley st, pick up and knit 33 (36, 39) sts along selvedge of square and mark first st as a peak st; rep from once more, k33 (36, 39) live sts and mark first st as a valley st—210 (228, 246) sts.

Row 2: With MC, CO 12 sts at beg of row, purl to end—222 (240, 258) sts.

Row 3: Change to CC3. Ssk, *knit to 2 sts before valley st, ssk, k1 (valley st), k2tog, knit to peak st, M1, k1 (peak st), M1; rep from * once more, knit to 2 sts before valley st, ssk, k1 (valley st), k2tog, knit to last 2 sts, k2tog—4 sts dec'd.

Row 4: With CC3, knit.

Row 5: Change to MC and rep Row 3—4 sts dec'd.

Row 6: With MC, purl.

Rows 7–14: Rep Rows 3–6 two more times—198 (216, 234) sts; 7 two-row stripes completed: 4 St st stripes with MC, 3 garter st stripes with CC3. Break yarn.

SQUARES TIER 3

Square 1: With RS facing, sl the first 33 (36, 39) sts of rnd, and join CC2 to first valley st. Work as for Square 2 of Tier 1.

Square 2: Work as for Square 2 of Tier 1, using CC3.

Square 3: Work as for Square 2 of Tier 1, using CC2.

MITERED STRIPE 3

Place sts of Tier 3 on longer cir needle with RS facing—99 (108, 117) sts; there will gaps between the group of sts. Join MC.

Row 1: (RS) With MC, pick up and knit 1 st from selvedge of Row 14 of Mitered Stripe 2, k33 (36, 39) live sts, *pick up and knit 2 sts in corner and mark first picked-up st as a peak st, pick up and knit 31 (34, 37) sts along selvedge of square, k1 and mark this st as a valley st, k32 (35, 38); rep from * once more, pick up and knit 2 sts in corner and mark first picked-up st as a peak st, pick up and knit 31 (34, 37) sts along selvedge of square, pick up and knit 1 st from selvedge of Row 14 in Mitered Stripe 2—200 (218, 236) sts total.

Row 2: With MC, purl.

Row 3: Change to CC3. Pick up and knit 1 st from selvedge of next CC3 stripe, *knit to peak st, M1, k1 (peak st), M1, knit to 2 sts before valley st, ssk, k1 (valley st), k2tog; rep from * once more, knit to peak st, M1, k1 (peak st), M1, knit to end, pick up and knit 1 st from selvedge of next CC3 stripe—4 sts inc'd.

Row 4: With CC3, knit.

Row 5: Change to MC, and rep Row 3, picking up 1 st at each side from selvedge of next MC stripe—4 sts inc'd.

Row 6: With MC, purl.

Rows 7–14: Rep Rows 3–6 two more times—224 (242, 260) sts; 7 two-row stripes completed: 4 St st stripes with MC, 3 garter st stripes with CC3. Break yarn.

SQUARES TIER 4

Place 13 sts at each end of row on holders—198 (216, 234) sts rem.

Square 1: With RS facing, join CC2 to first st on needle. Work basic garter st square over 33 (36, 39) sts without joining any sts. Place sts on holder.

Squares 2 and 3: With RS facing, sl the next 33 (36, 39) sts without working them, join CC3 to beg of next group of 33 (36, 39) sts. Work as for Square 2 of Tier 1. Place sts on holder.

Square 4: On empty straight needle, CO 22 (24, 26) sts with CC2 and 11 (12, 13) sts with CC1. Turn. *Next row:* (WS) Knit to last st, working sts with their same color, join last st to st at end of mitered stripe sts on needle using ssk. Complete as for Square 2 of Tier 1. Place sts on holder.

UPPER BACK
MITERED STRIPE 2

Place sts of Squares 5, 6, and 1 of Tier 2 on longer cir needle with RS facing for back—99 (108, 117) sts total; there will be gaps between the group of sts. Join MC to beg of selvedge of Square 4 of Tier 2, at top point of square. Work as for Mitered Stripe 2 of upper front.

SQUARES TIER 3, MITERED STRIPE 3, AND SQUARES TIER 4

Work as for upper front. Break yarn. Place sts on holder or waste yarn.

SHOULDER YOKE
MITERED STRIPE 4

Place sts from Squares 2, 3, and 4 of front and back Tier 4 on longer cir needle with RS facing; leave sts of both front and back Square 1 on holder—198 (216, 234) sts total; there will be gaps between the groups of sts. Join MC to beg of selvedge of Square 1 of upper back Tier 4, at top point of square. Using the knitted method, CO 12 sts onto left-hand needle for back right shoulder.

Rnd 1: (RS) With MC, knit first CO st and mark this st as a valley st, k11 rem CO sts, pick up and knit 33 (36, 39) sts along selvedge of square, *k33 (36, 39) live sts and mark first st as a valley st, pick up and knit 33 (36, 39) sts along selvedge of square and mark first st as a peak st,* rep from * to * once more, k33 (36, 39) live sts and mark first st as a valley st, use backward loop method to CO 12 sts for left back shoulder, CO 1 st and mark this st as a valley st, CO 11 sts for left front shoulder, pick up and knit 33 (36, 39) sts along selvedge of square, rep from * to * 2 times, k33 (36, 39) live sts and mark first st as a valley st, use backward loop method to CO 12 sts for right front shoulder—444 (480, 516) sts total: 4 peak sts, 8 valley sts, 4 center sections each on front and back with 32 (35, 38) sts between marked sts, 2 shoulder sections at each side of front and back with 44 (47, 50) sts between marked sts. Pm and join for working in the rnd; rnd begins with marked valley st in center of right shoulder.

Rnd 2: With MC, knit.

Rnd 3: Change to CC3. K1 (valley st at right shoulder), k2tog, *knit to 2 sts before valley st, ssk, k1 (valley st), k2tog, knit to peak st, M1, k1 (peak st), M1,* rep from * to * once more, knit to 2 sts before valley st, ssk, k1 (valley st), k2tog, knit to 2 sts before valley st, ssk, k1 (valley st at left shoulder), k2tog, rep from * to * 2 times, knit to 2 sts before valley st, ssk, k1 (valley st), k2tog, knit to last 2 sts, ssk—8 sts dec'd.

Rnd 4: With CC3, purl.

Rnd 5: Change to MC and rep Row 3—8 sts dec'd.

Rnd 6: With MC, knit.

Rnds 7–14: Rep Rows 3–6 two more times—396 (432, 468) sts: 4 peak sts, 8 valley sts, 12 sections with 32 (35, 38) sts between marked sts; 7 two-row stripes completed:

4 St st stripes with MC, and 3 garter st stripes with CC3. Break yarn.

SHOULDER TRIANGLES

Place first 66 (72, 78) sts of rnd for right back shoulder on shorter cir needle. Join CC2 to first st of right back shoulder with RS facing.

Row 1: (RS) With CC2, *k1, k2tog, k27 (30, 33), ssk, k1; join MC and rep from * once more, twisting yarns at color change to avoid leaving a hole—62 (68, 74) sts rem: 31 (34, 37) sts in each color section.

Row 2: Knit all sts with their same colors.

Row 3: With CC2, *k1, k2tog, knit to last 3 sts of color section, ssk, k1; with MC, rep from * once more—4 sts dec'd total: 2 sts dec'd in each color section.

Row 4: Knit all sts with their same colors.

Cont to work all sts with their same colors, rep the last 2 rows 11 (12, 14) more times, then work Row 3 once more—10 (12, 10) sts rem: 5 (6, 5) sts in each section. Knit 1 WS row, dec 0 (1, 0) st(s) in each section—10 sts rem: 5 sts in each section. *Next row:* *K1, k3tog, k1; rep from * once more—6 sts rem: 3 sts in each section. Knit 1 WS row. On the foll row, work k3tog 2 times with their same color—2 sts rem. Break yarns and fasten off rem sts. Place last 66 (72, 78) sts of rnd for right front shoulder on shorter cir needle. Join CC2 to first st of right front shoulder with RS facing, and work another two-tone shoulder triangle in the same manner. Place center 66 (72, 78) sts each for center back and front on separate holders. Place last 66 (72, 78) sts for left back shoulder on shorter cir needle, join CC2 to first st of left back shoulder with RS facing, and work another two-tone shoulder triangle. Place rem 66 (72, 78) sts for left front shoulder on shorter cir needle, join CC2 to first st of left front shoulder with RS facing, and work another two-tone shoulder triangle. With yarn threaded on a tapestry needle, sew front and back triangles tog at shoulders.

COLLAR

Beg at center front, place 132 (144, 156) sts of front and back neck opening on shorter cir needle with RS facing. Check that the lower edge slit is positioned at the back, unless you would prefer it in the front. Join MC with RS facing to right front. Collar is worked back and forth in rows of mitered garter st, using a different color for each section, and twisting yarns at color changes to avoid leaving holes.

Row 1: (RS) With MC, k33 (36, 39), join CC2 and k33 (36, 39), join second ball of MC and k33 (36, 39), join second ball of CC2 and k33 (36, 39).

Row 2: Knit all sts with their same colors.

Row 3: *For MC section, k1, k2tog, knit to last st of color section, M1, k1; for CC2 section, k1, M1, knit to last 3 sts of section, ssk, k1; rep from * once more.

Row 4: Knit all sts with their same colors.

Rep Rows 3 and 4 until collar measures 1¾" (4.5 cm), measured straight up from the shoulder, ending with a WS row. Fill in the valleys for mitered sections of collar separately as foll:

RIGHT FRONT

Using MC and working on 33 (36, 39) sts of right front section only, work as foll:

Row 1: (RS) K1, k2tog, knit to last 3 sts of MC section, k2tog, k1, turn—2 sts dec'd.

Row 2: (WS) Knit to end, turn.

Rep the last 2 rows 12 (13, 15) times, then work Row 3 once more—5 (6, 5) sts rem. Knit 1 WS row, dec 0 (1, 0) st(s)—5 sts rem. *Next row:* *K1, k3tog, k1—3 sts rem. Knit 1 WS row. On the foll row, k3tog—1 st rem. Break yarn and draw through last st.

LEFT FRONT

Using CC2 and working on 33 (36, 39) sts of left front section only, work as for right front.

CENTER BACK

Using MC and CC2 as established, work as for shoulder triangle over rem 66 (72, 78) sts of center back neck.

LEFT SLEEVE

Place 13 held sts of Mitered Stripe 3 at left front armhole on shorter cir needle, and join MC with RS facing. Sleeve is worked back and forth in rows of mitered garter st as foll:

Set-up row: (RS) K1 and mark this st as an edge st, k12, pick up and knit 33 (36, 39) sts along selvedge of Square 1 of Tier 4 and mark the first st as a valley st, place 33 (36, 39) live sts of same square on left-hand needle, k33 (36, 39) and mark the first st as a peak st, pick up and knit 1 st in corner and mark it as a valley st, pick up and knit 12 sts along CO for Mitered Stripe 4, pick up and knit 1 st in center of CO for stripe and mark it as a peak st, pick up and knit 12 sts along rem CO edge of stripe, pick up and knit 33 (36, 39) sts along selvedge of Square 4 of Tier 4 for upper back and mark the first st as a valley st, pick up and knit 33 (36, 39) sts along base of same square and mark the first st as a peak st, pick up and knit 1 st in corner and mark it as a valley st, place 13 held sts of Mitered Stripe 3 on left-hand needle, k12, k1 and mark last st as edge st—185 (197, 209) sts total: 3 peak sts, 4 valley sts, 1 edge st at each side, 2 center sections with 12 sts each, 4 sections with 32 (35, 38) sts each, 2 edge sections with 12 sts each. Knit 1 WS row. Cont in mitered garter st as foll:

Row 1: (RS) K1 (edge st), M1, *knit to 2 sts before valley st, ssk, k1 (valley st), k2tog, knit to peak st, M1, k1 (peak st), M1; rep from * 2 more times, knit to 2 sts before valley st, ssk, k1 (valley st), k2tog, knit to edge st, M1, k1 (edge st).

Row 2: Knit.

Rows 3–6: Rep Rows 1 and 2 twice more.

Row 7: (Dec Row 1) Extra decs for shaping are made in this row by working double decs, either k3tog or sssk (see Glossary, page 140), in each of the 32 (35, 38)-st sections. K1 (edge st), M1, knit to 2 sts before valley st, ssk, k1 (valley st), *k3tog, knit to peak st, M1, k1 (peak st), M1, knit to 3 sts before valley st, sssk,* k1 (valley st), k2tog, knit to peak st, M1, k1 (center peak st), M1, knit to 2 sts before valley st, ssk, k1 (valley st), rep from * to * once more, k1 (valley st), k2tog, knit to edge st, M1, k1 (edge st)—4 sts dec'd: each 32 (35, 38)-st section has 1 st dec'd, 12-st sections and marked sts rem unchanged.

Rows 8 and 10: Knit.

Rows 9 and 11: Rep Row 1.

Row 12: Knit.

Rep the last 6 rows (Row 7 foll by 5 rows worked even) 19 (22, 25) more times—105 sts rem for all sizes: 3 peak sts, 4 valley sts, 1 edge st at each side, 8 sections with 12 sts each; 128 (146, 164) rows completed including pick-up row and first WS row; piece measures about 11¾ (13¼, 15)" (30 [33.5, 38] cm) from pick-up, measured straight up along peak st at center of sleeve (do not measure along selvedges). Cont as foll:

Row 1: (Dec Row 2; RS) K1 (edge st), M1, *knit to 2 sts before valley st, sssk, k1 (valley st), k3tog, knit to peak st, M1, k1 (peak st), M1; rep from * 2 more times, knit to 2 sts before valley st, sssk, k1 (valley st), k3tog, knit to edge st, M1, k1 (edge st)—8 sts dec'd; 97 sts rem for all sizes: 3 peak sts, 4 valley sts, 1 edge st at each side, 8 sections with 11 sts each.

Row 2: Knit.

Row 3: K1 (edge st), M1, *knit to 2 sts before valley st,

ssk, k1 (valley st), k2tog, knit to peak st, M1, k1 (peak st), M1; rep from * 2 more times, knit to 2 sts before valley st, ssk, k1 (valley st), k2tog, knit to edge st, M1, k1 (edge st).

Row 4: Knit.

Rows 5 and 6: Rep Rows 3 and 4 once more.

Row 7: Rep Row 1 (Dec Row 2) once more—8 sts dec'd; 89 sts rem for all sizes: 3 peak sts, 4 valley sts, 1 edge st at each side, 8 sections with 10 sts each.

Row 8: Knit—piece measures about 12½ (14, 15¾)" (31.5 [35.5, 40] cm) from pick-up, measured straight up along peak st at center of sleeve (do not measure along selvedges). Rep Rows 3 and 4 without further decs until piece measures 16 (16½, 16½)" (40.5 [42, 42] cm) from pick-up, measured straight up along peak st at center of sleeve (do not measure along selvedges), or desired length. Break off MC.

CUFF TRIANGLES

With RS facing, join CC2. Fill in the valleys for mitered sections of lower sleeve separately as foll:

Row 1: (RS) K1, ssk, k7, k2tog, turn.

Row 2: K10.

Row 3: K1, ssk, knit to last st before turning gap in previous row, k2tog (last st of triangle tog with 1 st joined from next group), turn—1 st dec'd in triangle.

Row 4: Knit to end.

Rows 5–16: Rep Rows 3 and 4 six more times—3 triangle sts rem.

Row 17: K1, k3tog, turn—2 triangle sts rem.

Row 18: Knit.

Row 19: K1, k3tog, turn—2 triangle sts.

Row 20: K2tog—1 triangle st rem. Break yarn and fasten off last st—67 sleeve sts rem.

Work 2 more triangles the same—23 sts rem. Because of the edge st, there is 1 extra st for the last triangle. Work Row 1 of last triangle, then dec extra st on next row by working WS Row 2 as k8, ssk. Work Rows 3–20 as for other triangles. Break yarn and fasten off last st.

RIGHT SLEEVE

Place 13 held sts of Mitered Stripe 3 at right back armhole on shorter cir needle and join MC with RS facing. Work as for left sleeve.

FINISHING

With yarn threaded on a tapestry needle, sew sleeve and armhole gusset seams. Weave in loose ends. Block sweater or carefully steam-press on WS under a damp cloth.

The bold pattern of dark, medium, and light shades in the yoke of this sweater imitates pieced or strip-woven fabric, another African classic. The sweater begins with the V-shaped yoke, which is worked in modular units that build one upon the other. Then the lower body and pseudo-cuffed sleeves are worked outward from the yoke in mitered garter-stitch sections that reflect the strong diagonal lines of the modular units. Instructions are provided for adding an optional stand-up collar.

MATERIALS

SIZES 47 (51)" (119.5 [129.5] cm) finished chest/bust circumference. Shown in size 47" (119.5 cm) with heathered lilac neckband and in size 51" (129.5 cm) with periwinkle neckband.

YARN About 250 (325) g of a dark color (D), 150 (200) g of a medium color (M), 75 (100) g of a light color (L), and 50 (50) g of an accent color (A) of fingering-weight (CYCA Super Fine #1) yarn.

Shown here: Isager Tvinni (100% merino lambswool 558 yd [510 m]/100 g): #30 black (D), 3 (4) skeins.

For size 47": #23s gray heather (M), 2 skeins; #6s taupe heather (L) and #52s rose heather (A), 1 skein each.

For size 51": #42 charcoal (M), 2 skeins; #32 light gray heather (L) and #53 royal blue, 1 skein each.

Note: Accent color is used for V-neck insert and is not needed for stand-up collar version.

NEEDLES U.S. sizes 1 and 2 (2.5 and 3 mm): 24" (60 cm) circular (cir). Adjust needle size if necessary to obtain the correct gauge.

NOTIONS Stitch markers (m); removable markers or safety pins; stitch holders; spare double-pointed needle (dpn) to match larger size cir; tapestry needle.

GAUGE 27 sts and 54 rows = 4" (10 cm) in garter st using larger needle; 10 (13) sts and 20 (26) rows for square garter-st block measures about 1½ (2)" (3.8 [5] cm) square using larger needle.

STITCH GUIDE
GARTER STRIPES PATTERN

Row 1: (RS) With L and RS facing, either knit across the sts on the needle or pick up and knit the indicated number of sts.

Row 2: (WS) With L, purl.

Rows 3–6: With M, knit 4 rows.

Row 7: With L, knit.

Row 8: With L, purl.

Rep Rows 3–8 two (three) more times—20 (26) rows completed; 4 (5) St st stripes in L; 3 (4) garter st stripes in M. Cont as indicated in directions.

4-BLOCK INTARSIA SQUARE
(worked over 20 [26] sts)
First tier:

Row 1: (RS) With M, either pick up and knit or knit across first 10 (13) sts on needle, twist yarns at color change to avoid leaving a hole, then with D either pick up and knit or knit across rem 10 (13) sts on needle—20 (26) sts.

Row 2: (WS) K10 (13) with D, twist yarns at color change, k10 (13) with M.

Row 3: K10 (13) with M, twist yarns at color change, k10 (13) with D.

Row 4: Rep Row 2.

Rep Rows 3 and 4 eight (eleven) more times—20 (26) rows completed.

Second tier:

Row 1: (RS) K10 (13) with D, twist yarns at color change, k10 (13) with M.

Row 2: (WS) K10 (13) with M, twist yarns at color change, k10 (13) with D.

Rep Rows 1 and 2 nine (twelve) more times—20 (26) rows completed for this tier; 40 (52) rows total; intarsia square should be 2 blocks wide and 2 blocks high, with colors alternating in checkerboard fashion.

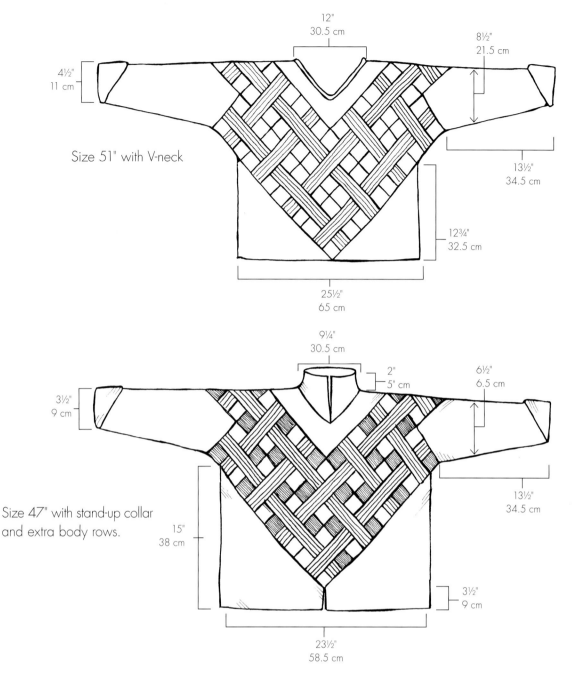

12"
30.5 cm

8½"
21.5 cm

4½"
11 cm

Size 51" with V-neck

13½"
34.5 cm

12¾"
32.5 cm

25½"
65 cm

9¼"
30.5 cm

2"
5" cm

6½"
6.5 cm

3½"
9 cm

Size 47" with stand-up collar
and extra body rows.

15"
38 cm

13½"
34.5 cm

3½"
9 cm

23½"
58.5 cm

NOTES

- To verify your gauge in pattern for the yoke, work Blocks 1–5 of yoke. Transfer the stitches temporarily to a length of scrap yarn. Dampen the piece and block it under hand towels until thoroughly dry. The piece should measure about 6 (8)" (15 [20.5] cm) wide and 3 (4)" (7.5 [10] cm) high. If correct, continue with the yoke. If not, adjust needle size and try again.

- Read about entrelac knitting on page 24. The one-piece yoke is composed of 146 blocks that are worked in order according to the diagram on page 39. Blocks build one upon the other in strips formed by stitches picked up along the edges of completed blocks, or by a combination of picked-up and live stitches as described in the instructions.

- On the diagram, the unshaded squares are blocks worked with the medium color (M), the shaded squares are blocks worked with the dark color (D), and the squares and rectangles with hatch marks are worked in garter stripes pattern (see Stitch Guide) with the light (L) and medium (M) colors.

- You may find it helpful to weave in the ends as you go, rather than have a large number of ends to weave in when finishing.

- When the yoke has been completed, stitches are picked up from the edges of the yoke with D and worked outward for the sleeves and lower body. The sleeves are worked in mitered garter stitch; the body is worked in garter stitch knit on the bias.

- The mitered garter stitch texture of the sleeves (as well as the optional stand-up collar) is created by working paired increases or decreases at marked points in order to make the garter stitch ridges run in zigzag lines.

YOKE

Block 1: With M and larger needle, CO 10 (13) sts. Knit 20 (26) rows—10 (13) garter ridges.

Block 2: Join L and work garter stripes patt (see Stitch Guide) for 20 (26) rows, working Row 1 by knitting across all sts with L.

Block 3: With D, knit 20 (26) rows—10 (13) garter ridges.

Block 4: With M, knit 20 (26) rows—10 (13) garter ridges. Place sts on holder to be worked later with Block 16.

Block 5: Rotate strip with Blocks 1–4 so left selvedge is uppermost, and Block 4 with held sts is at the right end of the strip. With L and RS facing, pick up and knit 40 (52) sts along left selvedge of strip (see illustration on page 39)—10 (13) sts each picked up from side of Blocks 4, 3, 2, and 1. Work 20 (26) rows in garter stripes patt, counting pick-up row as Row 1. With RS facing, place first 30 (39) sts on holder—10 (13) sts rem on needle. Check your gauge again at this point (see Notes, page 37).

Block 6: Rejoin D to beg of sts on needle with RS facing, knit 20 (26) rows—10 (13) garter ridges.

Block 7: With M, knit 20 (26) rows—10 (13) garter ridges.

Block 8: With M and L, work garter stripes patt for 20 (26) rows.

Block 9: With D, knit 20 (26) rows—10 (13) garter ridges.

Block 10: With M, knit 20 (26) rows—10 (13) garter ridges. Place sts on holder to be worked later with Block 32.

Block 11: Rotate strip with Blocks 6–10 so right selvedge is uppermost, and Block 10 with held sts is at the left end of the strip. With L and RS facing, pick up and knit 50 (65) sts along edge of strip—10 (13) sts picked up each from side of Blocks 6, 7, 8, 9, and 10; pick-up row counts as Row 1 of garter stripes patt. With RS facing, slip (sl) the last 10 (13) sts for Block 5 to dpn. Work Row 2 of garter stripes patt to last st, sl last st to end of dpn with sts of

Block 5, k2tog (last st of Block 11 tog with 1 st from Block 5). Turn, and work Row 3 of garter stripes patt. Cont in this manner, joining the edge of Block 11 to the live sts of Block 5 by knitting the last st of every WS row tog with 1 st from Block 5 dpn. When 20 (26) rows of garter stripe patt have been completed, all sts from Block 5 dpn have been joined. With RS facing, place last 30 (39) sts of Block 11 on holder—20 (26) sts rem on needle from Block 11.

Blocks 12–15: With M and D, work Row 1 of 4-block intarsia square (see Stitch Guide) over 20 (26) sts from Block 11. With RS facing, sl the rem 20 (26) held sts for Block 5 to dpn. Work Row 2 of 4-block intarsia square to last st, sl last st to end of dpn with sts of Block 5, k2tog (1 st of Block 12 tog with 1 st of Block 5). Cont in this manner, joining the edges of Blocks 12 and 14 to the live sts of Block 5 by knitting the last st of every WS row tog with 1 st from Block 5 dpn. When 40 (52) rows of 4-block intarsia square patt have been completed, all sts from Block 5 have been joined. Place 20 (26) sts at top of Blocks 14 and 15 on holder.

Block 16: With L and RS facing, knit across 10 (13) held sts from top of Block 4, pick up and knit 10 (13) sts from selvedge of Block 5, knit across 20 (26) held sts of Blocks 14 and 15—40 (52) sts. Cont in garter stripes patt, counting pick-up row as Row 1, until 20 (26) rows have been completed. With RS facing, place last 30 (39) sts on holder—10 (13) sts rem on needle.

Block 17: With D, knit 20 (26) rows—10 (13) garter ridges.

Block 18: With M, knit 20 (26) rows—10 (13) garter ridges.

Block 19: Join L and work garter stripes patt for 20 (26) rows, working Row 1 by knitting across all sts with L.

Blocks 20 and 21: Rep Blocks 17 and 18, in that order. Place sts on holder to be worked later with Block 56.

Block 22: With L and RS facing, pick up and knit 50 (65) sts along edge of Blocks 21, 20, 19, 18, and 17 as shown in diagram—10 (13) sts picked up from side of each block in strip; pick-up row counts as Row 1 of garter stripes patt. With RS facing, sl the next 10 (13) sts for Block 16 to dpn. Turn work. With WS facing, sl 1 st from Block 16

Dark

Medium

Light and medium stripes

dpn to main needle. Work Row 2 of garter stripes patt, working ssk (see Glossary, page 140) over first 2 sts (1 st of Block 16 dpn tog with 1 st of Block 22). Turn, work Row 3 of garter stripes patt. Cont in this manner, joining the edge of Block 22 to the live sts of Block 16 by working the first st of each WS row as ssk with 1 st from Block 16 dpn. When 20 (26) rows of garter stripe patt have been completed, all sts from Block 16 dpn have been joined. Place 50 (65) sts of Block 22 on holder.

Blocks 23–26: With RS facing, return 20 (26) rem sts of Block 16 to needle, and join M and D. Work Row 1 of 4-block intarsia square. With RS facing, sl the last 20 (26) held sts for Block 22 to dpn. Work Row 2 of 4-block intarsia square to last st, sl last st to end of dpn with sts of Block 22, k2tog (1 st of Block 23 tog with 1 st from Block 22). Cont in this manner, joining the edges of Blocks 23 and 25 to the live sts of Block 22 by knitting the last st of every WS row tog with 1 st from Block 22 dpn. When 40 (52) rows of 4-block intarsia square patt have been completed, all sts from Block 22 dpn have been joined. Place 20 (26) sts at top of Blocks 25 and 26 on holder.

Block 27: With L and RS facing, pick up and knit 50 (65) sts along edge of Blocks 26, 24, 16, 15, and 13—10 (13) sts picked up from side of each block in strip; pick-up row counts as Row 1 of garter stripes patt. With RS facing, sl the next 10 (13) sts for Block 11 to dpn. Turn work. With WS facing, sl 1 st from Block 11 dpn to main needle. Working ssk over first 2 sts (1 st of Block 11 dpn tog with 1 st of Block 27), work Row 2 of garter stripes patt. Turn, work Row 3 of garter stripes patt. Cont in this manner, joining the edge of Block 27 to the live sts of Block 11 by working the first st of each WS row as ssk with 1 st from Block 11 dpn. When 20 (26) rows of garter stripe patt have been completed, all sts from Block 11 dpn have been joined. With RS facing, place 50 (65) sts of Block 22 on holder.

Blocks 28–31: With RS facing, return 20 (26) rem sts of Block 11 to needle, and join M and D. Work Row 1 of 4-block intarsia square. With RS facing, sl the last 20 (26) held sts for Block 27 to dpn. Work Row 2 of 4-block intarsia square to last st, sl last st to end of dpn with sts of Block 27, k2tog (1 st of Block 28 tog with 1 st from Block 27). Cont in this manner, joining the edges of Blocks 28 and 30 to the live sts of Block 27 by knitting the last st of every WS row tog with 1 st from Block 27 dpn. When 40 (52) rows of 4-block intarsia square patt have been completed, all sts from Block 27 dpn have been joined. Place 20 (26) sts at top of Blocks 30 and 31 on holder.

Blocks 32–146: Cont to work joined blocks in this manner according to diagram until block 146 has been completed.

With M threaded on a tapestry needle, graft live sts of Block 146 to selvedge of Block 143 and sew any rem slits between blocks. Block piece to measure about 38 (51)" (96.5 [129.5] cm) high and 25½ (34)" (64.5 [86.5] cm) wide, from point to point.

NECK
V-NECK OPTION
With D, smaller needle, RS facing, and beg at corner where Blocks 64, 63, and 68 meet, *pick up and knit 1 st in corner, mark corner st with removable marker or safety pin, pick up and knit 60 (78) sts to next corner (10 [13] sts for each block); rep from * 3 more times—244 (316) sts. Join for working in the rnd, and place regular st marker on needle to mark beg of rnd. Change to A and knit 1 rnd, dec 2 sts at each corner as foll: *K1 (corner st), k2tog, knit to 2 sts before next marked corner st, k2tog; rep from * 3 more times—8 sts dec'd. Cont in garter st (purl 1 rnd, knit 1 rnd) for 25 (33) more rnds, dec 8 sts (2 sts at each corner) every knit rnd, ending with a purl rnd—140 (180) sts rem; neck insert measures about 1¾ (2½)" (4.5 [6.5] cm) from pick-up rnd. Change to M and work even in St st (knit all sts every rnd) for 6 rnds. BO all sts loosely, allowing BO edge to roll to outside.

STAND-UP COLLAR OPTION
With D and smaller needle, work pick-up rnd as for V-neck option—244 (316) sts. Join for working in the rnd, and place regular st marker on needle to mark beg of rnd. Change to M and knit 1 rnd, dec 2 sts at each corner as for V-neck option—8 sts dec'd. Cont in garter st (purl 1 rnd, knit 1 rnd), dec 8 sts (2 sts at each corner) every knit rnd for 27 (45) more rnds, ending with a purl rnd—132 sts rem; neck insert measures about 2 (3½)" (5 [7.9] cm) from pick-up rnd. Break yarn. Sl the first 33 sts without working them. Rejoin yarn to marked st at center front. Collar is worked back and forth in rows of mitered garter st as foll:

Row 1: (RS) K1 (marked st), k2tog, k30, M1 (see Glossary, page 140), k1 (marked st), M1, k30, ssk, k1 (marked st), k2tog, k30, M1, k1 (marked st), M1, k32 and mark last st of row with removable marker or safety pin—133 sts; 5 marked sts: 1 at each shoulder, 1 at center back, 2 on either side of front opening; 4 sections of 32 sts each between marked sts.

Row 2: (WS) Knit.

Row 3: *K1 (marked st), k2tog, k30, M1, k1 (marked st), M1, k30, ssk; rep from * once more, end k1 (marked st).

Rep Rows 2 and 3 until piece measures 2" (5 cm), measured straight up along one edge of neck slit from collar divide, ending with a WS row. Fill in the valleys of each mitered section of collar separately as foll:

Right front:

Row 1: (RS) K1 (marked st), k2tog, knit to 3 sts before next marked st, k2tog, k1, turn—2 sts dec'd.

Row 2: (WS) Knit to end, turn.

Row 3: K1 (marked st), k2tog, knit to 3 sts before turning gap in previous row.

Rep Rows 2 and 3 until 4 sts rem. On the next row, k2tog twice—2 sts rem. On the foll row, k2tog, cut yarn and draw through rem st.

Right back and Left back: For right back, rejoin yarn with RS facing to next group of sts and work as for right front. Rep over foll group of sts for left back.

Left front: Left front section has 1 extra st because 1 marked st was added at the left front edge when collar was divided. Work as for right front until 5 sts rem. On the foll row, k2tog, k1, k2tog—3 sts rem. On the foll row, k3tog, cut yarn, and draw through rem st. If desired, with M, smaller needle, and RS facing, pick up and knit 133 sts along now straight top edge of collar. Knit 4 rows. BO all sts loosely.

LEFT SLEEVE

Sleeve is worked back and forth in rows of mitered garter st; when shaping the sleeves, incs that would ordinarily occur at each end of the row are simply omitted as described below; this reduces the st count and tapers the sleeves without having to work any additional decs. With D, larger needle, RS facing, and beg at point of Block 57, pick up and knit 10 (13) sts each along edges of Blocks 57, 58, and 59; mark the first st picked up on Block 57 with removable marker or safety pin; pick up and knit 1 st in corner of Block 60 and mark picked-up corner st; pick up and knit 10 (13) sts each along edges of Blocks

knit to 2 sts before next marked st, ssk, k1 (marked st), k2tog, knit to end (no inc at end of row)—121 (157) sts rem. Work even in patt for 5 (3) rows. Rep the shaping of the last 6 (4) rows (dec row foll by 5 [3] rows worked even) 17 more times—87 (123) sts rem. Work dec row, then work 3 rows even—2 sts dec'd. Rep the shaping of the last 4 rows 8 (17) more times—69 (87) sts rem; 5 marked sts; 2 sections of 30 (39) sts between the marked sts in middle of sleeve; 2 sts rem between markers in sections at each end of row. Work even, if necessary, until sleeve measures about 13½" (34.5 cm) from armhole pick-up row (measured along selvedge) and 17½" (44.5 cm) from pick-up row, measured along the center marked column. *Note:* Sleeve ends in a point over the back of the hand (shown folded back in schematic). BO all sts, working incs and decs at marked positions as established in BO row.

RIGHT SLEEVE

With D, larger needle, RS facing, and beg at point of Block 137, pick up and knit 10 (13) sts each along edges of Blocks 137, 138, and 139; mark the first st picked up on Block 137 with removable marker or safety pin; pick up and knit 1 st in corner of Block 140 and mark picked-up corner st; pick up and knit 10 (13) sts each along edges of Blocks 141, 142, and 144; pick up and knit 1 st in outer corner of Block 144 and mark it; pick up and knit 10 (13) sts each along edges of Block 144, 145, and 146; pick up and knit 1 st in corner of Block 143 and mark it; pick up and knit 10 (13) sts each along edges of Blocks 49, 37, and 36; mark last st picked up—123 (159) sts total; 5 marked sts: 1 at each end of row, 1 each in corners of Blocks 140, 144, and 143; 2 sections of 30 (39) sts between marked sts in middle of sleeve; 1 section of 29 (38) sts between marked sts at each end of sleeve. Complete as for left sleeve.

LEFT FRONT BODY

With D, larger needle, RS facing, and beg at lower point of Block 1, pick up and knit 10 (13) sts each along edge of 11 (9) blocks, ending where Blocks 56 and 57 (Blocks 20 and 21) meet—110 (117) sts. Unattached blocks between body and sleeve will form underarm gussets. *Note:* Finished garment lengths from shoulder as shown are 22½ (25½)" (57 [65] cm). To compensate for its shorter yoke and achieve the desired length, size 47" has extra rows of D worked even at the lower edge. For a cropped version with a finished length of 19" (48.5 cm), these extra rows can be omitted. For cropped version of size 47" and for size 51",

61, 69, and 70; pick up and knit 1 st in outer corner of Block 70 and mark it; pick up and knit 10 (13) sts each along edges of Block 70, 71, and 72; pick up and knit 1 st in corner of Block 73 and mark it; pick up and knit 10 (13) sts each long edges of Blocks 74, 87, and 88; mark last st picked up—123 (159) sts total; 5 marked sts: 1 at each end of row, 1 each in corners of Blocks 60, 70, and 73; 2 sections of 30 (39) sts between marked sts in middle of sleeve; 1 section of 29 (38) sts between marked sts at each end of sleeve. Knit 1 WS row. Work mitered garter st patt as foll:

Row 1: (RS) K1, *M1, knit to 2 sts before next marked st, ssk, k1 (marked st), k2tog, knit to next marked st, M1, k1 (marked st); rep from * once more.

Row 2: (WS) Knit.

Next row: (RS) Dec 2 sts by omitting M1 incs at each end of row as foll: K1 (marked st), knit to 2 sts before next marked st (no inc at beg of row), ssk, k1 (marked st), k2tog, knit to next marked st, M1, k1 (marked st), M1, skip to *For all sizes* below. For 22½" (57 cm) long version of size 47", work as foll:

Row 1: (WS) K2tog, knit to last st, M1, k1.

Row 2: (RS) Knit.

Rep these 2 rows until piece measures 2½" (6.5 cm) from pick-up row measured at center, or about 3½" (9 cm) measured straight up from point of Block 1 along shaped edge, ending with a WS row.

For all sizes: Beg with the next RS row, work k2tog at beg of every row until 1 st rem—piece measures about 15 (12¾)" (38 [32.5] cm) from pick-up row, measured straight along edge that will become the side seam and 11½" (29 cm) for smaller cropped version. Cut yarn and fasten off last st.

RIGHT FRONT BODY

With D, larger needle, RS facing, and beg where Blocks 35 and 36 (Blocks 33 and 34) meet, pick up and knit 10 (13) sts along edge of 11 (9) blocks, ending at lower point of Block 1—110 (117) sts. For cropped version of size 47" and for size 51", skip to *For all sizes* below. For 22½" (57 cm)-long version of size 47", work as foll:

Row 1: (WS) Knit.

Row 2: (RS) K2tog, knit to last st, M1, k1.

Rep these 2 rows until piece measures 2½" (6.5 cm) from pick-up row measured at center, or about 3½" (9 cm) measured straight up from point of Block 1 along shaped edge, ending with a WS row.

For all sizes: Beg with the next RS row, work k2tog at beg of every row until 1 st rem—piece measures about 15 (12¾)" (38 [32.5] cm) from pick-up row, measured straight along edge that will become the side seam and 11½" (29 cm) for smaller cropped version. Cut yarn and fasten off last st.

LEFT BACK BODY

With D, larger needle, RS facing, and beg where Blocks 88 and 89 (Blocks 90 and 91) meet, pick up and knit 10 (13) sts along edge of 11 (9) blocks, ending at lower point of Block 109—110 (117) sts. Work as for right front body.

RIGHT BACK BODY

With D, larger needle, RS facing, and beg at lower point of Block 109, pick up and knit 10 (13) sts along edge of 11 (9) blocks, ending where Blocks 136 and 137 (Blocks 134 and 135) meet—110 (117) sts. Work as for left front body.

FINISHING

Block sweater to finished measurements. With yarn threaded on a tapestry needle and using the mattress st (see Glossary, page 141), sew sleeve and side seams; center front and back seams of lower edge extension of size 47" can be sewn closed or left open for slits as shown. Weave in loose ends. Wear with sleeve points folded up, if desired.

Peter Wath

Inspired by the small flashes of white visible on the backsides of leaping antelopes, the fronts of this kimono-style cardigan feature patterned panels that build around small white squares. The back of the cardigan and the pullover version (page 52) feature a mitered chevron pattern that is worked in a combination of garter stitch and stockinette stitch.

Natural History Museum, Århus

CARDIGAN

The panels are worked in mitered squares and triangles from lower front to shoulders, then joined at the back neck where they flow into the mitered chevron pattern of the back. Accent areas of stockinette stitch in contrasting colors emphasize the directionality of the mitered pieces. Stitches for the sides and sleeves are picked up along the edges of the fronts and back, then worked outward in rows for the shaped side panels and sleeves. Stitches for the combined neckband/lapels are picked up around the front opening, and the drapey lapels are shaped into points.

MATERIALS

SIZES 40½ (44½, 48½)" (103 [113, 123] cm) finished chest/bust circumference. Shown in size 44½" (113 cm).

YARN About 275 (325, 350) g each of two yarns held together for main color (MC), 275 g each of two yarns held together for contrasting color (CC), and 25 g of accent color (A) of fingering-weight (CYCA Super Fine #1) yarn.

Shown here: Isager Tvinni Alpaca (50% lambswool, 50% alpaca; 558 yd [510 m]/100 g): #30 black (MC), 3 (4, 4) skeins; #47 dark blue-gray (CC), 3 skeins.

Isager Spinni (100% pure new wool; 667 yd [610 m] 100 g): #30 black (MC), 3 (4, 4) skeins; #4s charcoal heather (CC), 3 skeins; #2s light gray heather (A), 1 skein.

Note: Use 1 strand each of Tvinni Alpaca and Spinni held together for MC and CC; use 2 strands of Spinni held together for A.

NEEDLES U.S. size 2 (3 mm): straight and 24" (60 cm) or 32" (80 cm) circular (cir). Adjust needle size if necessary to obtain the correct gauge.

NOTIONS Stitch markers (m); removable markers or safety pins; stitch holders; tapestry needle.

GAUGE 25 sts and 48 rows = 4" (10 cm) in garter st with MC (1 strand each of Tvinni Alpaca and Spinni held together).

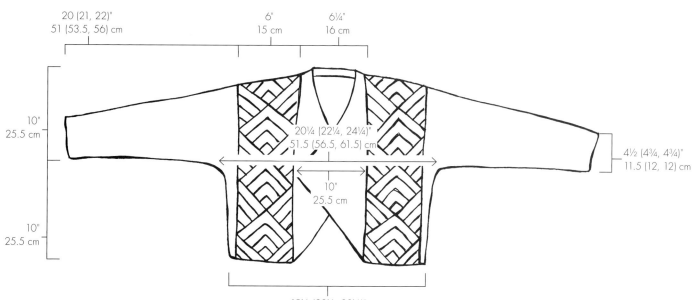

20 (21, 22)"
51 (53.5, 56) cm

6"
15 cm

6¼"
16 cm

10"
25.5 cm

20¼ (22¼, 24¼)"
51.5 (56.5, 61.5) cm

4½ (4¾, 4¾)"
11.5 (12, 12) cm

10"
25.5 cm

10"
25.5 cm

18¼ (20¼, 22¼)"
46.5 (51.5, 56.5) cm

NOTES

- MC and CC always refer to one strand each of Tvinni Alpaca and Spinni held together; A always refers to two strands of Spinni held together for the accent colored squares in the cardigan front panels.
- The mitered garter and stockinette pattern is created by working paired increases or decreases on either side of marked "peak" and "valley" stitches in order to make the garter-stitch ridges run in zigzag lines. Use removable markers or safety pins to mark these stitches as instructed, moving the markers up as you work.
- Although the schematic sketch and the way the garment is photographed make it look as if each lapel is only as wide as the front opening, just barely touching the edge of the front patterned panel, each lapel is actually about 3¾" (9.5 cm) wider than the opening, and will overlap front patterned panel when the garment is worn.

FRONT PANELS (MAKE 2)
LOWER FRONT TRIANGLE (MAKE 2)

With CC and straight needles, CO 2 sts.

Row 1: (RS) K1f&b (see Glossary, page 140) 2 times—4 sts.

Row 2: Knit.

Row 3: K1, M1 (see Glossary, page 140), knit to last st, M1, k1—2 sts inc'd.

Row 4: Knit.

Rows 5–10: Rep Rows 3 and 4 three more times—12 sts after Row 10.

Row 11: (RS) Change to MC. K1, M1, knit to last st, M1, k1—14 sts.

Row 12: Purl with MC.

Rows 13–22: Change to CC. Rep Rows 3 and 4 five more times, ending with a WS row—24 sts after Row 22.

Poul Valsted

Cut yarn, and place sts on holder. Make another triangle the same as the first, and leave sts on needle.

MITERED SQUARE

Slip (sl) 17 sts of triangle as if to purl (pwise) without working them. Join A to beg of rem 7 sts of same triangle. Work the small, rectangular accent color patch at lower corner of mitered square as foll: K6, temporarily sl last triangle st to right-hand needle. Place 24 held sts of second triangle on left-hand needle. Return slipped st to left-hand needle, ssk (last st of first triangle tog with first st of foll triangle), turn. *Next row:* (WS) Sl 1 CC st from right-hand needle to left-hand needle, with A, ssp (one A st and one CC st; see Glossary, page 140), p6, turn. *Next row:* (RS) With A, k6, ssk, turn. Rep the last 2 rows 2 more times, ending with a RS row—41 sts; 7 sts with A at center, 17 sts in triangle at each side; small 7-st, 7-row patch with A completed. Cut off A. Sl 7 sts of color A patch to left-hand needle pwise. Join CC with RS facing to base of patch.

Row 1: (RS) With CC, pick up and knit 7 sts along selvedge of patch, knit across first 6 sts of patch, ssk (last st of patch with next st of triangle), turn.

Row 2: K13, k2tog (last st of center short-row section with next st of triangle), turn—14 sts in short-rowed center section; 16 triangle sts at each side.

Row 3: K7, M1 and mark this stitch as a "peak" st, k6, ssk (last st of center short-row section with next st of triangle), turn—15 sts in center short-row section.

Row 4: K14, k2tog, turn—15 sts in center short-row section; 15 triangle sts at each side.

Row 5: Knit to peak st, M1, k1 (peak st), M1, knit to last st of center short-row section, ssk, turn.

Row 6: Knit to last st of center short-row section, k2tog, turn—17 sts in center short-row section; 14 triangle sts at each side.

Rows 7–10: Rep Rows 5 and 6 two times—21 sts in center short-row section, 12 triangle sts at each side after Row 10.

Row 11: Change to MC. Rep Row 5.

Row 12: With MC, purl to last st of center short-row section, p2tog, turn—23 sts in center short-row section, 11 triangle sts at each side.

Rows 13–22: Change to CC. Rep Rows 5 and 6 five times—33 sts in center short-row section, 6 triangle sts at each side after Row 22.

Rows 23 and 24: Change to MC. Rep Rows 11 and 12—35 sts in center short-row section, 5 triangle sts at each side.

Rows 25–32: Change to CC. Rep Rows 5 and 6 four times—43 sts in center short-row section, 1 triangle st at each side after Row 32.

Row 33: Rep Row 5—45 sts in center short-row section.

Row 34: Knit to last st of center short-row section, and *at the same time* inc 3 sts evenly across, k2tog—48 sts in center short-row section; all triangle sts have been joined. Cut yarn.

With RS facing, sl first 24 sts to holder, leaving last 24 sts of mitered square still on needle.

LEFT SIDE TRIANGLE

With WS facing, rejoin CC, and use the knitted method (see Glossary, page 139) to CO 2 sts onto end of needle closest to the lower front triangle—26 sts: 2 left side triangle sts, 24 mitered square sts. With WS still facing, k1, ssk (last side triangle st tog with 1 mitered square st), turn—2 side triangle sts; 23 mitered square sts.

Row 1: (RS) K1, M1, k1, turn—3 side triangle sts.

Row 2: K2, ssk, turn—3 side triangle sts, 22 mitered square sts.

Row 3: Knit to last st, M1, k1, turn—1 st inc'd for side triangle.

Row 4: Knit to last st of side triangle, ssk, turn—1 mitered square st joined.

Rows 5–8: Rep Rows 3 and 4 two more times—6 side triangle sts; 19 mitered square sts after Row 8.

Row 9: Change to MC. Rep Row 3—1 st inc'd for side triangle.

Row 10: With MC, purl to last st of side triangle, ssp, turn—1 mitered square st joined.

Rows 11–20: Change to CC. Rep Rows 3 and 4 five times—12 side triangle sts; 13 mitered square sts after Row 20.

Rows 21 and 22: Change to MC. Rep Rows 9 and 10.

Rows 23–32: Change to CC. Rep Rows 3 and 4 five times—18 side triangle sts; 7 mitered square sts after Row 32.

Rows 33–34: Change to MC. Rep Rows 9 and 10.

Rows 35–42: Change to CC. Rep Rows 3 and 4 four times—23 side triangle sts; 2 mitered square sts after Row 42.

Row 43: Rep Row 3.

Row 44: Knit to last st of side triangle, sssk (see Glossary, page 140), turn—24 side triangle sts; all mitered square sts have been joined. Cut yarn, and place st on holder.

RIGHT SIDE TRIANGLE

Return rem 24 held mitered square sts to needle. With RS facing, rejoin CC, and use the knitted method to CO 2 sts onto end of needle closest to lower front triangle—26 sts; 2 right side triangle sts, 24 mitered square sts.

Row 1: (RS) K1, k2tog (last side triangle st tog with 1 mitered square st), turn—2 side triangle sts; 23 mitered square sts.

Row 2: K2, turn.

Row 3: K1, M1, k2tog, turn—3 side triangle sts; 22 mitered square sts.

Row 4: K3, turn.

Row 5: K1, M1, knit to last st of side triangle, k2tog, turn—1 st inc'd for side triangle; 1 mitered square st joined.

Row 6: Knit.

Rows 7–10: Rep Rows 5 and 6 two more times—6 side triangle sts; 19 mitered square sts after Row 10.

Row 11: Change to MC. Rep Row 5—1 st inc'd for side triangle; 1 mitered square st joined.

Row 12: With MC, purl.

Rows 13–22: Change to CC. Rep Rows 5 and 6 five times—12 side triangle sts; 13 mitered square sts after Row 22.

Rows 23 and 24: Change to MC. Rep Rows 11 and 12.

Rows 25–34: Change to CC. Rep Rows 5 and 6 five times—18 side triangle sts; 7 mitered square sts after Row 34.

Rows 35–36: Change to MC. Rep Rows 11 and 12.

Rows 37–44: Change to CC. Rep Rows 5 and 6 four times—23 side triangle sts; 2 mitered square sts after Row 46.

Row 45: K1, M1 knit to last st of side triangle, k3tog, turn—24 side triangle sts; all mitered square sts have been joined.

Row 46: Knit to end. Leave sts on needle. Cut yarn.

*Work mitered square over live sts of side triangles, then work left side triangle and right side triangle once more; rep from * once more—2 lower front triangles, 3 mitered squares, and 3 each right and left side triangles completed. Work mitered square once more—front panel measures about 20" (51 cm) from beg, measured along selvedge (do not measure up the center of the panel), and about 6" (15 cm) wide. Cut yarn, and place 48 sts of last mitered square on holder. Make a second front panel the same as the first.

BACK PANEL
BACK NECK TRIANGLE

With CC and straight needles, CO 5 sts. Knit 1 row, turn.

Row 1: (RS) [K1, M1] 2 times, k1 and mark this st as a peak st, [M1, k1] 2 times—9 sts.

Row 2: Knit.

Row 3: K1, M1, knit to peak st, M1, k1 (peak st), M1, knit to last st, M1, k1—4 sts inc'd.

Row 4: Knit.

Rows 5–10: Rep Rows 3 and 4 three more times—25 sts after Row 10.

Row 11: Change to MC. Rep Row 3—4 sts inc'd.

Row 12: Purl with MC.

Rows 13–22: Change to CC. Rep Rows 3 and 4 five more times—49 sts after Row 22.

Cut yarn. Place sts on holder.

JOINING ROW

With RS facing, place held sts of front panels on needle with back neck triangle in between them—145 sts; 48 sts each front panel; 49 back neck triangle sts in center. Join MC, ready to work a RS row. K1, k2tog, k20, M1, k1 (front panel peak st), M1, k20, k2tog, k1, k2tog (last st of front panel and first st of back neck triangle) and mark this st as a "valley" st, k1, k2tog, k20, M1, k1 (back neck triangle peak st), M1, k20, k2tog, k1, k2tog (last st of back neck triangle and first st of front panel) and mark this st as a valley st, k1, k2tog, k20, M1, k1 (front panel peak st), M1, k20, k2tog, k1—143 sts; 3 marked peak sts, 2 marked valley sts, 23 sts each in 6 sections. Purl 1 WS row with MC. Work mitered garter and St st patt as foll:

Row 1: (RS) Change to CC. K1, k2tog, *knit to peak st, M1, k1 (peak st), M1, knit to 2 sts before valley st, k2tog, k1 (valley st), k2tog; rep from * once more, knit to peak st, M1, k1 (peak st), M1, knit to last 3 sts, k2tog, k1.

Row 2: Knit.

Rows 3–10: Rep Rows 1 and 2 four more times.

Row 11: Change to MC. Rep Row 1.

Row 12: Purl with MC.

Rep these 12 rows 10 more times; then work Rows 1–10 once more. Including 2-row MC stripe at joining row, there will be a total of twelve 2-row MC stripes and twelve 10-row (5 garter ridge) CC stripes worked from end of mitered squares—piece measures about 20" (51 cm) from beg of back neck triangle, measured straight up along column of peak sts at center back, and about 18¼" (46.5 cm) wide.

LEFT LOWER BACK TRIANGLE

With RS facing, use the knitted method to CO 2 sts with CC onto end of needle.

Row 1: (RS) K1, k2tog (last CO st tog with 1 back st), turn—2 triangle sts; 22 sts rem before next marked peak st.

Row 2: K2, turn.

Row 3: K1, M1, k2tog, turn—3 triangle sts; 21 sts rem before peak st.

Row 4: K3, turn.

Row 5: K1, M1, knit to last triangle st, k2tog, turn—1 st inc'd for side triangle; 1 back st joined.

Row 6: Knit.

Rows 7–10: Rep Rows 5 and 6 two more times—6 triangle sts; 18 sts rem before peak st after Row 10.

Row 11: Join MC. Rep Row 5—1 st inc'd for side triangle; 1 back st joined.

Row 12: With MC, purl. Cut off MC.

Rows 13–22: Change to CC. Rep Rows 5 and 6 five times—12 triangle sts; 12 sts rem before peak st after Row 22.

Row 23: Join MC. K1, k2tog, knit to last triangle st, k2tog, turn—11 triangle sts; 11 sts rem before peak st.

Row 24: With MC, purl. Cut off MC.

Row 25: Change to CC. K1, k2tog, knit to last triangle st, k2tog, turn—1 st dec'd for triangle; 1 back st joined.

Row 26: Knit.

Rows 27–34: Rep Rows 25 and 26 four more times—6 triangle sts, 6 sts rem before peak st after Row 34.

Rows 35 and 36: Join MC. Rep Rows 23 and 24—5 triangle sts; 5 sts rem before peak st. Cut off MC

Rows 37–40: Rep Rows 25 and 26 two more times—3 triangle sts; 3 sts rem before peak st after Row 40.

Row 41: K2, k2tog, turn—3 triangle sts; 2 sts rem before peak st.

Rows 42 and 44: Knit.

Row 43: K1, k2tog (last 2 triangle sts), k2tog (2 sts before peak st), turn—2 triangle sts; 1 st rem before peak st.

Row 45: K2tog (2 triangle sts), k2tog (next st tog with peak st), turn.

Row 46: K2tog, cut yarn and fasten off last st.

LARGE LOWER BACK TRIANGLE

Join MC to rem 119 back sts on needle with RS facing.

Row 1: (RS) K1, k2tog, k20, k2tog (valley st tog with foll st), turn—23 triangle sts; 22 sts rem before next marked peak st.

Row 2: With MC, purl. Cut off MC

Row 3: Change to CC. K1, k2tog, knit to last triangle st, k2tog, turn—22 triangle sts; 21 sts rem before peak st.

Row 4: Knit.

Rows 5–12: Rep Rows 3 and 4 three more times—19 triangle sts; 18 sts rem before peak st after Row 12.

Row 13: Join MC. K1, k2tog, knit to last triangle st, k2tog—1 triangle st dec'd; 1 back st joined.

Row 14: With MC, purl. Cut off MC.

Rows 15–24: Change to CC. Rep Rows 3 and 4 five times—13 triangle sts; 12 sts rem before peak st after Row 24.

Rows 25 and 26: Join MC. Rep Rows 13 and 14—1 triangle st dec'd; 1 back st joined. Cut off MC.

Rows 27–36: Change to CC. Rep Rows 3 and 4 five times—7 triangle sts; 6 sts rem before peak st after Row 36.

Rows 37 and 38: Join MC. Rep Rows 13 and 14—6 triangle sts; 5 sts rem before peak st. Cut off MC.

Rows 39–44: Rep Rows 3 and 4 three more times—3 triangle sts; 2 sts rem before peak st after Row 44.

Row 45: K1, k2tog (last 2 triangle sts), k2tog (2 sts before peak st), turn—2 triangle sts; 1 st rem before peak st.

Row 46: Knit.

Row 47: K2tog (2 triangle sts), k2tog (next st tog with peak st), turn.

Row 48: K2tog, cut yarn and fasten off last st.

Join MC to rem 71 back sts on needle with RS facing. Work another large lower back triangle—23 back sts rem.

RIGHT LOWER BACK TRIANGLE

With WS facing, rejoin CC and use the knitted method to CO 2 sts onto end of needle (side edge of piece)—25 sts; 2 triangle sts, 23 back sts. With WS still facing, k1, ssk, turn—2 triangle sts; 22 back sts.

Row 1: (RS) K1, M1, k1, turn—3 triangle sts.

Row 2: K2, ssk, turn—3 triangle sts, 21 back sts.

Row 3: Knit to last st, M1, k1, turn—1 st inc'd for triangle.

Row 4: Knit to last st of triangle, ssk, turn—1 back st joined.

Rows 5–8: Rep Rows 3 and 4 two more times—6 triangle sts; 18 back sts after Row 8.

Row 9: Join MC. Rep Row 3—1 st inc'd for triangle.

Row 10: With MC, purl to last st of triangle, ssp, turn—1 back st joined.

Rows 11–20: Change to CC. Rep Rows 3 and 4 five times—12 triangle sts; 12 back sts after Row 20.

Row 21: Change to MC. Knit to last 2 sts, k2tog, turn—1 triangle st dec'd.

Row 22: With MC, purl to last st of triangle, ssp, turn—1 back st joined.

Row 23: Change to CC. Knit to last 2 sts, k2tog, turn—1 triangle st dec'd.

Row 24: Knit to last st of triangle, ssk, turn—1 back st joined.

Rows 25–32: Rep Rows 23 and 24 four more times—6 triangle sts; 6 back sts after Row 24.

Rows 33 and 34: Change to MC. Rep Rows 21 and 22—5 triangle sts; 5 back sts.

Rows 35–40: Change to CC. Rep Rows 23 and 24 three more times—2 triangle sts; 2 back sts.

Row 41: K2tog, turn—1 triangle st; 2 back sts.

Row 42: K1, ssk, turn—2 sts.

Row 43: K2tog, cut yarn, and fasten off last st.

LEFT SIDE AND SLEEVE

With MC, cir, RS facing, and beg at side edge of left front, pick up and knit 125 sts along selvedge to shoulder, then pick up and knit 125 sts from shoulder to lower edge of back—250 sts total. Knit 1 WS row—1 garter ridge completed. Knit 0 (12, 24) rows—1 (7, 13) garter ridge(s) completed.

SHAPE SIDES

Cont in garter st, BO 13 sts at beg of next 6 rows, then BO 12 sts at beg of next 4 rows—124 sts rem; 12 (24, 36) rows completed including pick-up row; 6 (12, 18) garter ridges; piece measures 1 (2, 3)" (2.5 [5, 7.5] cm) from base of pick-up row.

SHAPE SLEEVE

Cont in garter st, dec 1 st at each end of needle every 6 rows 28 (14, 14) times, then every 7 rows 6 (18, 18) times—56 (60, 60) sts rem; sleeve measures about 17½" (44.5 cm) from last BO row for sides. Work even in garter st for another 1½" (3.8 cm)—sleeve measures about 19" (48.5 cm) from last BO row for sides; entire sleeve/side piece measures about 20 (21, 22)" (51 [53.5, 56] cm) from base of pick-up row. BO all sts.

RIGHT SIDE AND SLEEVE

With MC, cir, RS facing, and beg at side edge of right back, pick up and knit 125 sts along selvedge to shoulder, then pick up and knit 125 sts from shoulder to lower edge of front—250 sts total. Work as for left side and sleeve.

NECKBAND AND FRONT LAPELS

With MC, cir, RS facing, and beg at lower edge of right front opening, pick up and knit 118 sts along selvedge to shoulder, pm, pick up and knit 38 sts across back neck, pm, pick up and knit 118 sts from shoulder to lower edge of left front opening—274 sts total. *Next row:* (WS) Sl 1 pwise, k1, k2tog, knit to end—1 st dec'd. Rep the last row 11 more times, ending with a RS row—262 sts rem; piece measures about 1" (2.5 cm) from pick-up row. *Next row:* (WS) Sl 1 pwise, k1, k2tog, knit to marker, remove marker, join second ball of MC, BO 38 back neck sts, remove second marker, knit to end. *Next row:* (RS) Sl 1 pwise, k2, k2tog, work to end of first group of sts, knit across second group of sts—2 groups of 111 sts each. *Next row:* Working each side separately, work every row across sts for each group as foll: Sl 1 pwise, k1, k2tog, knit to end—1 st dec'd from each group. Rep the last row 107 more times—3 sts rem in each group; neckband/lapel piece measures about 10" (25.5 cm) from pick-up row. For each group, work k3tog, cut yarn, and fasten off last st.

FINISHING

With yarn threaded on a tapestry needle, weave in ends at lower edges, using yarn tails to neaten and straighten the points of the mitered pattern st. With yarn threaded on a tapestry needle, sew sleeve and side seams. Weave in loose ends. Block sweater or carefully steam-press on WS under a damp cloth.

PULLOVER

In this pullover version of the cardigan on page 44, the same two-color, mitered garter-stitch chevron pattern is used on both the front and back. The patterned panels are worked from the lower edge to the shoulder. The front and back are joined at the shoulders, then stitches are picked up along the edges and worked outward for the tapered side panels and sleeves. The stand-up collar follows the shape of the mitered pattern at the front neck.

MATERIALS

SIZES 38 (40, 44, 48, 52)" (96.5 [101.5, 112, 122, 132] cm) finished chest/bust circumference. Shown in size 44" (112 cm).

YARN About 250 (275, 325, 350, 400) g each of two yarns held together for main color (MC) and 325 (350, 350, 375, 375) g contrasting color (CC) of fingering-weight (CYCA Super Fine #1) yarn.

Shown here: Isager Tvinni Alpaca (50% lambswool, 50% alpaca; 558 yd [510 m]/100 g): #30 black (MC), 3 (3, 4, 4, 4) skeins.

Isager Spinni (100% pure new wool; 667 yd [610 m]/100 g): #30 black (MC), 3 (3, 4, 4, 4) skeins

Isager Highland (100% pure new wool; 612 yd [560 m]/100 g): #10 sage blue (CC), 4 (4, 4, 4, 4) skeins.
Note: Use one strand each of Tvinni Alpaca and Spinni held together for MC, and a single strand of Highland for CC.

NEEDLES U.S. size 2 (3 mm): straight and 24" (60 cm) or 32" (80 cm) circular (cir). Adjust needle size if necessary to obtain the correct gauge.

NOTIONS Stitch markers (m); removable markers or safety pins; stitch holders; tapestry needle.

GAUGE 25 sts and 48 rows in garter st = 4" (10 cm) with MC (1 strand each of Tvinni Alpaca and Spinni held together).

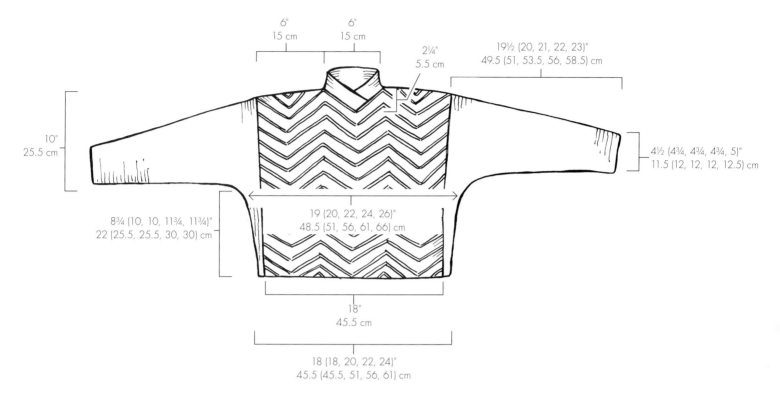

6"
15 cm

6"
15 cm

2¼"
5.5 cm

19½ (20, 21, 22, 23)"
49.5 (51, 53.5, 56, 58.5) cm

10"
25.5 cm

4½ (4¾, 4¾, 4¾, 5)"
11.5 (12, 12, 12, 12.5) cm

8¾ (10, 10, 11¾, 11¾)"
22 (25.5, 25.5, 30, 30) cm

19 (20, 22, 24, 26)"
48.5 (51, 56, 61, 66) cm

18"
45.5 cm

18 (18, 20, 22, 24)"
45.5 (45.5, 51, 56, 61) cm

NOTES

- MC always refers to one strand each of Tvinni Alpaca and Spinni held together; CC always refers to a single strand of Highland.
- The mitered garter and stockinette pattern is created by working paired increases or decreases on either side of marked "peak" and "valley" stitches in order to make the garter-stitch ridges run in zigzag lines. Use removable markers or safety pins to mark these sts as instructed, moving the markers up as you work.

BACK

LOWER SIDE TRIANGLE (MAKE 2)

With CC and straight needles, CO 2 sts.

Row 1: (RS) K1f&b (see Glossary, page 140) 2 times—4 sts.

Row 2: Knit.

Row 3: K1, M1 (see Glossary, page 140), knit to last st, M1, k1—2 sts inc'd.

Row 4: Knit.

Rows 5–10: Rep Rows 3 and 4 three more times—12 sts after Row 10.

Row 11: (RS) Change to MC. K1, M1, knit to last st, M1, k1—14 sts.

Row 12: Purl with MC.

Rows 13–22: Change to CC. Rep Rows 3 and 4 five more times, ending with a WS row—24 sts after Row 22.

Cut yarn and place sts on holder. Make another triangle the same as the first.

LOWER CENTER TRIANGLES (MAKE 2)

With CC and straight needles, CO 5 sts. Knit 1 row, turn.

Row 1: (RS) [K1, M1] 2 times, k1 and mark this st as a "peak" st, [M1, k1] 2 times—9 sts.

Row 2: Knit.

Row 3: K1, M1, knit to peak st, M1, k1 (peak st), M1, knit to last st, M1, k1—4 sts inc'd.

Row 4: Knit.

Rows 5–10: Rep Rows 3 and 4 three more times—25 sts after Row 10.

Row 11: Change to MC. Rep Row 3—4 sts inc'd.

Row 12: Purl with MC.

Rows 13–22: Change to CC. Rep Rows 3 and 4 five more times—49 sts after Row 22.

Cut yarn and place sts on holder. Make another triangle the same as the first.

JOIN TRIANGLES

With RS facing, place triangles on straight needle in this order: 1 lower side triangle, 2 lower center triangles, 1 lower side triangle—146 sts total. Join MC, ready to work a RS row. K1, M1, k21, k2tog, use backward loop method (see Glossary, page 139) to CO 1 st and mark new st as a "valley" st, *k2tog, k22, M1, k1 (peak st), M1, k22, k2tog, use backward loop method to CO 1 st and mark new st as a valley st; rep from * once more, k2tog, k21, M1, k1—149 sts: 2 marked peak sts, 3 marked valley sts, 24 sts each in 6 sections. Purl 1 WS row with MC. Work mitered garter and St st patt as foll:

Row 1: (RS) Change to CC. K1, M1, *knit to 2 sts before valley st, k2tog, k1 (valley st), k2tog, knit to peak st, M1, k1 (peak st), M1; rep from * once more, knit to 2 sts before valley st, k2tog, k1 (valley st), k2tog, knit to last st, M1, k1.

Row 2: Knit.

Rows 3–10: Rep Rows 1 and 2 four more times.

Row 11: Change to MC. Rep Row 1.

Row 12: Purl with MC.

Rep these 12 rows 12 (13, 13, 14, 14) more times. Beg with 2-row MC joining-row stripe and counting straight up along the center valley st, there will be a total of 14 (15, 15, 16, 16) 2-row MC stripes and 13 (14, 14, 15, 15) 10-row (5 garter ridge) CC stripes—piece measures about 18¾ (20, 20, 21¾, 21¾)" (47.5 [51, 51, 55, 55] cm) from beg, measured along selvedge, and about 18" (45.5 cm) wide. Break yarn. Place first 49 sts on holder for right back shoulder, place next 51 sts on holder for center back neck—49 sts rem on needle for left back shoulder.

SHOULDER TRIANGLES

Row 1: (RS) Change to CC. Cont on 49 left back shoulder sts as foll: K1, k2tog, knit to 2 sts before valley st, k2tog, k1 (valley st), k2tog, knit to last 3 sts, k2tog, k1—4 sts dec'd.

Row 2: Knit.

Rows 3–10: Rep Rows 1 and 2 four more times—29 sts after Row 10.

Row 11: Change to MC. Rep Row 1—4 sts dec'd.

Row 12: Purl with MC.

Rep Rows 1–8 once more—9 sts rem after Row 8. *Next row:* (RS) K1, k2tog, k3tog, k2tog, k1—5 sts rem. Knit 1 row. Change to MC. *Next row:* (RS) K1, k3tog, k1—3 sts rem. Knit 1 row. K3tog, cut yarn, and fasten off last st.

Return 49 held sts for right back shoulder to needle. Join CC with RS facing, and work as for left back shoulder triangle.

CENTER BACK TRIANGLE

Return 51 held center back neck sts to needle. Join CC with RS facing. Work Row 1 of shoulder triangle—47 sts. *Next row:* (WS) K1, k2tog, knit to last 3 sts, k2tog, k1—45 sts. Beg with Row 3, complete as for shoulder triangle.

FRONT

Work as for back until both shoulder triangles have been completed, leaving 51 sts on holder for center front.

JOIN SHOULDERS

With MC, cir needle, and RS facing, pick up and knit 37 sts along left back shoulder. With MC, straight needle, and RS facing, pick up and knit 37 sts along left front shoulder. Turn work carefully inside out, and with right sides touching each other, use three-needle bind-off technique (see Glossary, page 140) and other end of cir needle to join left shoulders tog. Repeat for right shoulder.

LEFT SIDE AND SLEEVE

With MC, cir needle, RS facing, and beg at side edge of left front, pick up and knit 118 (125, 125, 136, 136) sts along selvedge to shoulder, then pick up and knit 118 (125, 125, 136, 136) sts from shoulder to lower edge of back—236 (250, 250, 272, 272) sts total. Knit 1 WS row—1 garter ridge completed. Knit 0 (0, 12, 24, 36) rows—1 (1, 7, 13, 19) garter ridge(s) completed.

SHAPE SIDES

Cont in garter st, BO 28 (13, 13, 15, 15) sts at beg of next 4 (6, 6, 8, 8) rows, then BO 0 (12, 12, 14, 14) sts at beg of next 0 (4, 4, 2, 2) rows—124 sts rem; 6 (12, 24, 36, 48) rows completed including pick-up row, 3 (6, 12, 18, 24) garter ridges; piece measures ½ (1, 2, 3, 4)" (1.3 [2.5, 5, 7.5, 10] cm) from base of pick-up row.

SHAPE SLEEVE

Cont in garter st, dec 1 st at each end of needle every 6 rows 28 (14, 14, 14, 7) times, then every 7 rows 6 (18, 18, 18, 24) times—56 (60, 60, 60, 62) sts rem; sleeve measures about 17½" (44.5 cm) from last BO row for sides. Work even in garter st for another 1½" (3.8 cm)—sleeve measures about 19" (48.5 cm) from last BO row for sides; entire sleeve/side piece measures about 19½ (20, 21, 22, 23)" (49.5 [51, 53.5, 56, 58.5] cm) from base of pick-up row. BO all sts.

RIGHT SIDE AND SLEEVE

With MC, cir needle, RS facing, and beg at side edge of right back, pick up and knit 118 (125, 125, 136, 136) sts along selvedge to shoulder, then pick up and knit 118 (125, 125, 136, 136) sts from shoulder to lower edge of back—236 (250, 250, 272, 272) sts total. Work as for left side and sleeve.

FINISHING
COLLAR

Place 25 sts of right front neck edge on cir needle, leaving 26 sts for left front neck (including valley st at center front) on holder. Join CC with RS facing, knit 25 right front neck sts to shoulder, pick up and knit 38 sts across back neck, place rem 26 neck sts on straight needle with RS facing, and use cir needle to knit to last 2 sts, k2tog—88 sts total. Do not join. *Next row:* Sl 1 pwise, knit to end. Rep the last row 28 more times, ending with a WS row—collar measures about 2¼" (5.5 cm). BO all sts.

With yarn threaded on a tapestry needle, weave in ends at lower edges, using yarn tails to neaten and straighten the points of the mitered pattern st. With yarn threaded on a tapestry needle, sew sleeve and side seams. Weave in loose ends. Block sweater or carefully steam-press on WS under a damp cloth.

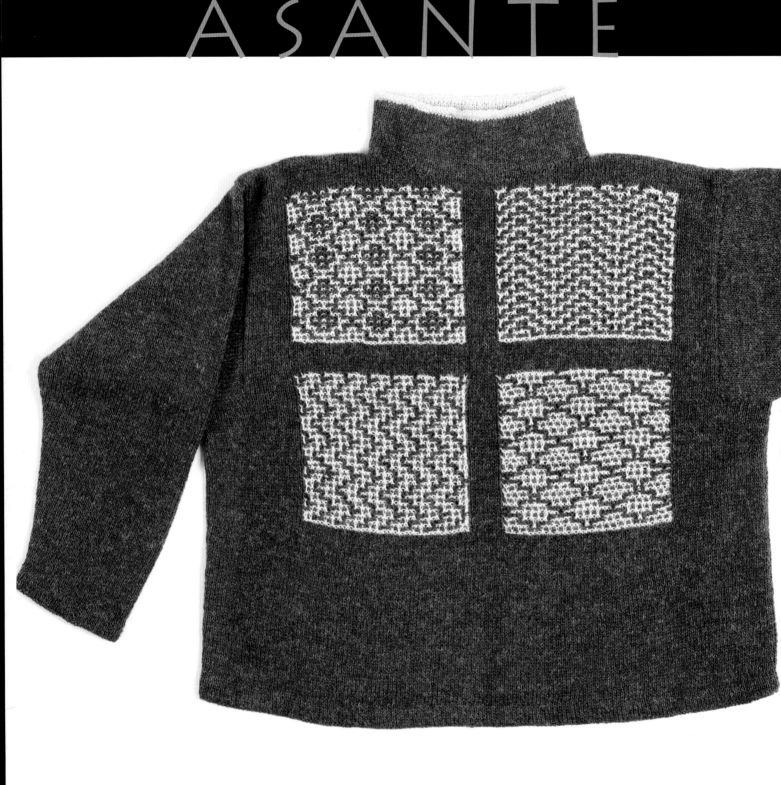

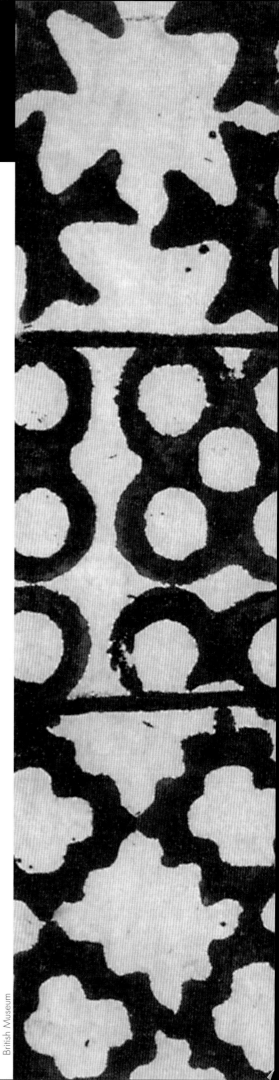

The geometric blocks in this sweater were inspired by a collage of patterns printed on cloth by the Asante people in Ghana. The front and back are worked in stockinette stitch from the lower hemmed edge to the shoulders. Knitted in garter stitch, four different blocks of intarsia slip-stitch motifs decorate the center front; another block decorates the upper back. To prevent the garter-stitch motifs from drawing in vertically, there are extra short-rows in each motif— four rows are worked for each motif for every two rows worked for the rest of the body. The sleeves are fashioned in stockinette stitch from the hemmed lower edges to the notched armholes. A stand-up collar, worked double thickness (gray on the outside, white on the inside), is topped off with a tiny rolled edge.

MATERIALS

SIZES 40½ (44, 48)" (103 [112, 122] cm) finished chest/bust circumference. Shown in size 48" (122 cm).

YARN About 200 (225, 250) g each of two colors held together for main color (MC), and 50 (50, 50) g contrasting color (CC) of fingering-weight (CYCA Super Fine #1) yarn.

Shown here: Isager Tvinni Alpaca (50% lambswool, 50% alpaca; 558 yd [510 m]/100 g): #4s charcoal heather (MC), 2 (3, 3) skeins; #0 natural white (CC), 1 skein.

Isager Spinni (100% pure new wool; 667 yd [610 m]/100 g): #47 dark blue-gray (MC), 2 (2, 3) skeins.

Note: Use 1 strand each of Tvinni Alpaca and Spinni held together for MC; use a single strand of Tvinni Alpaca for CC.

NEEDLES U.S. sizes 2 and 4 (3 and 3.5 mm): 16" (40 cm) and 24" (60 cm) circular (cir). Adjust needle size if necessary to obtain the correct gauge.

NOTIONS Stitch markers (m); stitch holders; tapestry needle.

GAUGE 25 sts and 34 rows = 4" (10 cm) in St st with MC (1 strand each of Tvinni Alpaca and Spinni held together) using larger needles; 45 sts = 7" (18 cm) wide in slip-stitch patt from charts using larger needles.

NOTES

- MC always refers to a double strand of Tvinni Alpaca and Spinni held together; CC always refers to a single strand of Tvinni Alpaca.

- Read about intarsia knitting on page 71. The slip-stitch panels are worked with separate balls of contrasting color (CC), intarsia-style. The main color (MC) is used across every row from selvedge to selvedge. Twist the yarns at the color changes on either side of slip-stitch panels to avoid leaving holes.

- When working the chart patterns, slip stitches as if to purl with the unused color carried along the wrong side of the work. In other words, on the right-side rows slip as if to purl with yarn in back, and on wrong-side rows slip as if to purl with yarn in front; slipped strands should never float across the right side of the fabric.

- The color used for each pair of rows is indicated in brackets at the side of each chart.

- The slip-stitch patterns have a different row gauge from the surrounding stockinette areas. To introduce the necessary extra rows, chart rows worked with CC are worked back and forth over the stitches of the slip-stitch panel *only*, without working the surrounding MC stockinette background stitches.

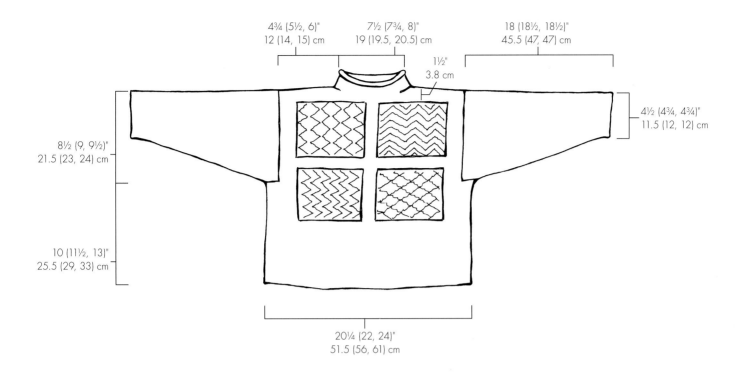

Measurements shown on schematic:

4¾ (5½, 6)"
12 (14, 15) cm

7½ (7¾, 8)"
19 (19.5, 20.5) cm

18 (18½, 18½)"
45.5 (47, 47) cm

1½"
3.8 cm

4½ (4¾, 4¾)"
11.5 (12, 12) cm

8½ (9, 9½)"
21.5 (23, 24) cm

10 (11½, 13)"
25.5 (29, 33) cm

20¼ (22, 24)"
51.5 (56, 61) cm

BACK

With MC and smaller 24" (60 cm) cir needle, CO 126 (138, 150) sts. Do not join into a rnd. Knitting the first and last st of every row for selvedge sts, work center 124 (136, 148) sts in St st until piece measures ¾" (2 cm) from CO edge, ending with a RS row. Knit across the next WS row for turning ridge. Change to larger 24" (60 cm) cir needle. Maintaining selvedge sts, work even in St st until piece measures 10 (11½, 13)" (25.5 [29, 33] cm) from turning ridge, ending with a WS row.

SHAPE ARMHOLES

BO 10 (11, 13) sts at beg of next 2 rows—106 (116, 124) sts rem. Re-establish selvedge sts, and work even in St st until armholes measure 3 (3½, 4)" (7.5 [9, 10] cm), ending with a RS row. Work the next WS row as foll: K1 (selvedge st), p39 (44, 48), place marker (pm), p13, M1 as if to purl (see Glossary, page 140), p13, pm, p39 (44, 48), k1 (selvedge st)—107 (117, 125) sts, 27 sts center sts between markers.

SET UP CENTER BACK PANEL

(RS) With MC work to first marker, drop MC to WS, slip marker (sl m), join CC, knit 27 center sts with CC, turn, knit back across 27 center sts on WS with CC, drop CC to WS, turn.

Row 1: (RS) Pick up MC where it was dropped at beg of panel. With MC, work Row 1 of Back chart (page 60; see Notes, page 58, regarding how to slip sts) across 27 center sts, sl m, work to end.

Row 2: (WS) With MC, work to marker, sl m, work Row 2 of chart across center 27 sts, sl m, work to end.

Row 3: (RS) With MC, work to marker, drop MC to WS, sl m, with CC work Row 3 of chart across 27 center sts, turn.

Row 4: (WS) With CC, work Row 4 of chart across 27 center sts, drop CC to WS, turn.

Row 5: (RS) Pick up MC where it was dropped at beg of panel. With MC, work Row 5 of chart across 27 center sts, sl m, work to end.

Row 6: (WS) With MC, work to marker, sl m, work Row 6 of chart across 27 center sts, sl m, work to end.

Row 7: (RS) With MC, work to marker, drop MC to WS, sl m, with CC work Row 7 of chart across 27 center sts, turn.

Row 8: (WS) With CC, work Row 8 of chart across 27 center sts, drop CC to WS, turn.

Row 9: (RS) Pick up MC where it was dropped at beg of panel. With MC, work Row 1 of chart across 27 center sts, sl m, work to end.

Row 10: (WS) With MC, work to marker, sl m, work Row 2 of chart across 27 center sts, sl m, work to end.

MC: knit on RS

MC: knit on WS

MC: slip on both RS and WS

CC: knit on RS

CC: knit on WS

CC: slip on both RS and WS

pattern repeat

Chart 1

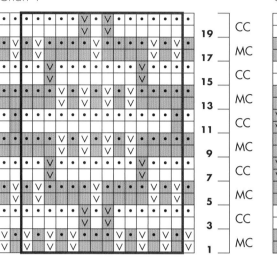

	CC
19	
	MC
17	
	CC
15	
	MC
13	
	CC
11	
	MC
9	
	CC
7	
	MC
5	
	CC
3	
	MC
1	

Chart 2

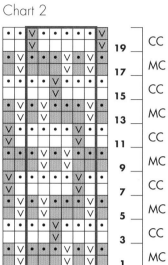

	CC
19	
	MC
17	
	CC
15	
	MC
13	
	CC
11	
	MC
9	
	CC
7	
	MC
5	
	CC
3	
	MC
1	

Chart 3

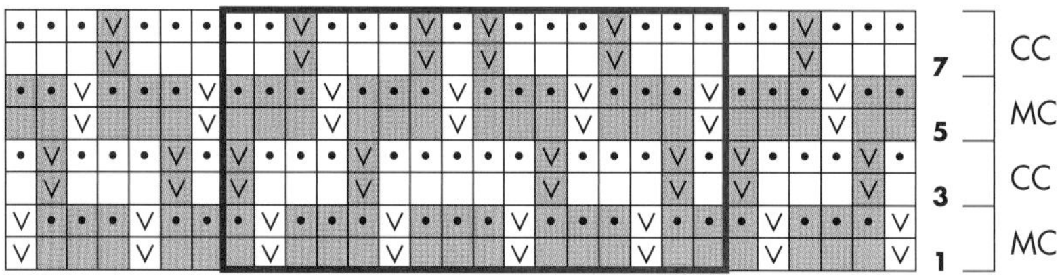

	CC
7	
	MC
5	
	CC
3	
	MC
1	

Chart 4

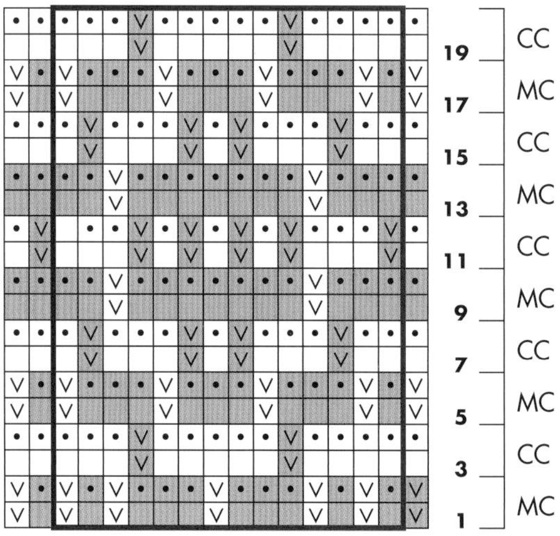

	CC
19	
	MC
17	
	CC
15	
	MC
13	
	CC
11	
	MC
9	
	CC
7	
	MC
5	
	CC
3	
	MC
1	

Back

	CC
7	
	MC
5	
	CC
3	
	MC
1	

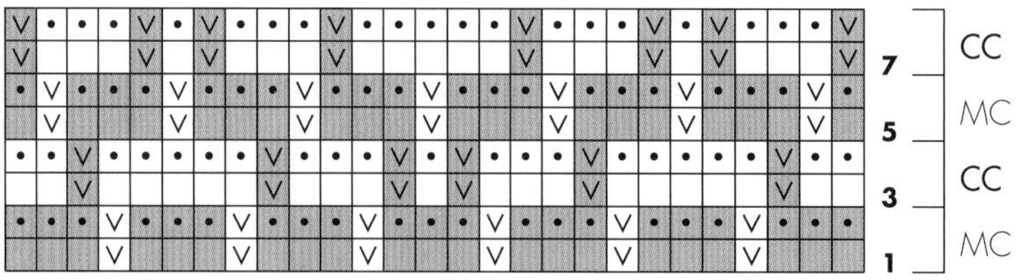

Cont in this manner, working charted rows with CC over 27 center sts only, and working MC rows from selvedge to selvedge, until Rows 1–8 of Back chart have been worked a total of 8 times, then work Rows 1 and 2 of chart once more—66 chart rows completed; 68 panel rows completed total, counting the 2 set-up rows worked with CC; panel measures about 4¼" (11 cm) high. Break off CC. On the next row, work across all sts with MC, dec 1 st at center—106 (116, 124) sts. Work even with MC in St st until armholes measure 8½ (9, 9½)" (21.5 [23, 24] cm), ending with a WS row. Place sts on holder.

FRONT

With MC and smaller 24" (60 cm) cir needle, CO 126 (138, 150) sts. Work as for back until piece measures 3½ (5½, 7½)" (9 [14, 19] cm) from turning ridge, ending with a RS row. Work the next WS row as foll: K1 (selvedge st), p13 (19, 25), pm, p45, pm, p8, pm, p45, pm, p13 (19, 25), k1 (selvedge st)—2 marked groups of 45 sts with 8 sts in between them at center front. Cont as foll, knitting the selvedge sts every row, working the first and last 13 (19, 25) sts in St st, working the 8 sts bet panels in St st, and working the marked groups of 45 sts in slip-st patt as indicated:

SET UP CHARTS 1 AND 2

(RS) With MC work to first marker, sl m, join CC, knit first group of 45 marked sts with CC, turn, knit back across 45 marked sts on WS with CC, and drop CC to WS. Turn. With RS facing, slip (sl) to second group of marked sts without working any sts, join second ball of CC, knit second group of 45 marked sts with CC, turn, knit back across 45 marked sts on WS with CC, and drop CC to WS. Turn. With RS facing, sl sts without working them to beg of first panel.

Row 1: (RS) Pick up MC where it was dropped at beg of first panel. With MC, work Row 1 of Chart 1 across first group of 45 marked sts, sl m, k8, sl m, work Row 1 of Chart 2 across second group of 45 marked sts, sl m, work to end.

Row 2: (WS) With MC, work to marker, sl m, work Row 2 of Chart 2 across next 45 sts, sl m, p8, sl m, work Row 2 of Chart 1 across next 45 sts, sl m, work to end.

Rows 3 and 4: With MC, work to first marker, drop MC to WS, sl m, with CC work Row 3 of Chart 1 across next 45 sts, turn, work Row 4 of Chart 1 back across same 45 sts, turn. With RS facing, sl without working any

sts to second group of 45 sts. With CC, work Row 3 of Chart 2 across next 45 sts, turn, work Row 4 of Chart 2 back across same 45 sts, turn. With RS facing, sl sts without working them to beg of first panel.

Row 5: (RS) Pick up MC where it was dropped at beg of first panel. With MC, work Row 5 of Chart 1 across 45 sts, sl m, k8, sl m, work Row 5 of Chart 2 across 45 sts, sl m, work to end.

Row 6: (WS) With MC, work to marker, sl m, work Row 6 of Chart 2 across 45 sts, sl m, p8, sl m, work Row 6 of Chart 1 across 45 sts, sl m, work to end.

Rows 7 and 8: With MC, work to first marker, drop MC to WS, sl m, with CC work Row 7 of Chart 1 across next 45 sts, turn, work Row 8 of Chart 1 back across same 45 sts, turn. With RS facing, sl without working any sts to second group of 45 sts. With CC, work Row 7

of Chart 2 across next 45 sts, turn, work Row 8 of Chart 2 back across same 45 sts, turn. With RS facing, sl sts without working them to beg of first panel.

Row 9: (RS) Pick up MC where it was dropped at beg of first panel. With MC, work Row 9 of Chart 1 across 45 sts, sl m, k8, sl m, work Row 9 of Chart 2 across 45 sts, sl m, work to end.

Row 10: (WS) With MC, work to marker, sl m, work Row 10 of Chart 2 across 45 sts, sl m, p8, sl m, work Row 10 of Chart 1 across 45 sts, sl m, work to end.

Cont in this manner, working charted rows with CC over marked 45-st groups and working MC rows from selvedge to selvedge with 8 sts in St st between panels. *Note:* Armhole shaping takes place while the panels are still in progress; read the next section all the way through before proceeding. Cont in patts until Rows 1–20 of charts have been worked a total of 4 times, then work Rows 1–16 of charts once more—96 chart rows completed; 98 panel rows completed total, counting the 2 set-up rows worked with CC; panels measure about 6¼" (16 cm) high. *At the same time:* When piece measures 10 (11½, 13)" (25.5 [29, 33] cm) from turning ridge, ending with a WS row, shape armhole as foll:

SHAPE ARMHOLE

BO 10 (11, 13) sts at beg of next 2 rows—106 (116, 124) sts rem. Re-establish selvedge sts, and work even in patts until panels have been completed. Break off CC. Work even with MC only for 1¼" (3.2 cm) above end of panels, ending with a WS row and leaving markers in the work.

SET UP CHARTS 3 AND 4

(RS) Work set-up the same as for Charts 1 and 2. Turn. With RS facing, sl sts without working them to beg of first panel.

Row 1: (RS) Pick up MC where it was dropped at beg of first panel. With MC, work Row 1 of Chart 3 across first group of 45 marked sts, sl m, k8, sl m, work Row 1 of Front Chart 4 across second group of 45 marked sts, sl m, work to end.

Row 2: (WS) With MC, work to marker, sl m, work Row 2 of Chart 4 across next 45 sts, sl m, p8, sl m, work Row 2 of Front Chart 3 across next 45 sts, sl m, work to end.

Rows 3 and 4: With MC, work to first marker, drop MC to WS, sl m, with CC work Row 3 of Chart 3 across next 45 sts, turn, work Row 4 of Chart 3 back across same 45 sts, turn, with RS facing, sl without working any sts to second group of 45 sts. With CC, work Row 3 of Chart 4 across next 45 sts, turn, and work Row 4 of Chart 4 back across same 45 sts, turn. With RS facing, sl sts without working them to beg of first panel.

Row 5: (RS) Pick up MC where it was dropped at beg of first panel. With MC, work Row 5 of Chart 3 across 45 sts, sl m, k8, sl m, work Row 5 of Chart 4 across 45 sts, sl m, work to end.

Row 6: (WS) With MC, work to marker, sl m, work Row 6 of Chart 4 across 45 sts, sl m, p8, sl m, work Row 6 of Chart 3 across 45 sts, sl m, work to end.

Cont in this manner, working charted rows with CC over marked 45-st groups and working MC rows from selvedge to selvedge, including the 8 sts in St st between panels. Cont in patt until Rows 1–8 of Chart 3 have been worked a total of 11 times, then work Rows 1–4 of Chart 3 once more; and until Rows 1–20 of Chart 4 have been worked a total of 4 times, then work Rows 1–12 of Chart 4 once more—92 chart rows completed; 94 panel rows completed total, counting the 2 set-up rows worked with CC; panels measure about 6" (15 cm) high). Break off CC. Work even with MC only until armholes measure 7 (7½, 8)" (18 [19, 20.5] cm), ending with a WS row.

SHAPE FRONT NECK

Work 45 (49, 52) sts, place center 16 (18, 20) sts on holder, join second ball of yarn, work to end—45 (49, 52) sts at each side. Working each side separately, at each neck edge BO 5 sts once, then BO 3 sts 3 times, then BO 1 st—30 (34, 37) sts at each side. Work even, if necessary, until armholes measure 8½ (9, 9½)" (21.5 [23, 24 cm]), ending with a WS row. Place sts on holder.

SLEEVES

With MC and smaller 16" (40 cm) cir needle, CO 56 (60, 60) sts. Do not join into a rnd. Knitting the first and last st of every row for selvedge sts, work center 54 (58, 58) sts in St st until piece measures ¾" (2 cm) from CO edge, ending with a RS row. Knit across the next WS row for turning ridge. Change to larger 16" (40 cm) cir needle. Maintaining selvedge sts, work even in St st until piece measures ¾" (2 cm) from turning ridge, ending with a

WS row. Beg with the next RS row, inc 1 st at each end of needle inside selvedge sts every 6 rows 13 (11, 5) times, then every 4 rows 12 (15, 24) times—106 (112, 118) sts; piece measures about 15½" (39.5 cm) from turning ridge. Work even until piece measures 18 (18½, 18½)" (45.5 [47, 47] cm) from turning ridge. BO all sts.

FINISHING
JOIN SHOULDERS

Place 30 (34, 37) sts each for front and back left shoulders on ends of larger 24" (60 cm) cir needle. Turn work carefully inside out, and with right sides touching, use the three-needle bind-off technique (see Glossary, page 140) and other larger cir needle to join left shoulders tog. Rep for right shoulder. Leave rem 46 (48, 50) sts at center back neck on holder.

NECKBAND

Place 46 (48, 50) held back neck sts on larger 16" (40 cm) cir needle, and join MC with RS facing. Work across 46 (48, 50) back neck sts in St st, pick up and knit 56 (58, 60) sts along shaped front neck edge—102 (106, 110) sts. Pm and join for working in the rnd. Work even in St st until neckband measures 2¾" (7 cm) from pick-up rnd, or desired length.

Facing: Change to smaller 16" (40 cm) cir needle and purl 1 rnd for turning ridge. Change to CC, and work even in St st until neckband measures 2¾" (7 cm) from turning ridge. BO all sts loosely.

Rolled edge: With smaller 16" (40 cm) cir needle, CC, and RS facing, pick up and knit 102 (106, 110) sts along purl "bumps" of turning ridge. Pm and join for working in the rnd. Work even in St st for 6 rnds. BO all sts.

With yarn threaded on a tapestry needle, sew sleeves into armholes. Sew sleeve and side seams. Fold lower body hem, sleeve hems, and neckband facing to the inside along turning ridges and sew in place with yarn threaded on tapestry needle. Weave in loose ends. Carefully steam-press sweater under a damp cloth.

The pieced checkerboard fabric that inspired this sweater design (and hence its name) comes from Sierra Leone. The strip-look pattern in the sweater is achieved through wide bands of intarsia color blocks that repeat in an offset arrangement. The striped pattern is punctuated with garter-stitch slip-stitch motifs bordered with narrow bands of contrasting colors that echo the accent motifs in the woven fabric. A contrasting facing finishes off the inside of the mock-turtleneck collar.

MATERIALS

SIZES 43 (47, 52)" (109 [119.5, 132] cm) finished chest/bust circumference. Shown in size 47" (119.5 cm).

YARN About 250 (275, 300) g each of two colors held together for main color (MC), 50 (60, 75) g each of two colors held together for contrasting color (CC), 10–12 yd (m) each of 6 to 8 colors for accent stripes (A), and 35 yd (m) extra of one accent color for neckband facing of fingering-weight (CYCA Super Fine #1) yarn.

Shown here: Isager Tvinni Alpaca (50% lambswool, 50% alpaca; 558 yd [510 m]/100 g): #100 navy (MC), 3 skeins (all sizes); #0 natural white (CC), 1 skein.

Isager Spinni (100% pure new wool; 667 yd [610 m]/100 g): #101 thunder blue (MC), 3 skeins (all sizes); #2s light gray heather (CC), 1 skein.

Accent colors shown include Tvinni Alpaca and Spinni in #7s taupe heather, #16 teal, #24s orange heather, #25s plum heather, #39s peach heather, #43s olive heather, and #52s dusty rose heather.

Note: Use 1 strand each of Tvinni Alpaca and Spinni held together for MC and CC for St st sections, and a single strand of Tvinni Alpaca for CC in slip-stitch panels. For accent color stripes above and below slip-stitch panels, use a different combination of 2 strands of the same color or 1 strand each of 2 different colors held together.

NEEDLES U.S. sizes 2 and 4 (3 and 3.5 mm): 16" (40 cm) and 24" (60 cm) circular (cir). Adjust needle size if necessary to obtain the correct gauge.

NOTIONS Stitch markers (m); stitch holders; tapestry needle; yarn bobbins (optional) for working intarsia.

GAUGE 25 sts and 38 rows = 4" (10 cm) in St st with MC (1 strand each of Tvinni Alpaca and Spinni held together) using larger needles; 19 sts = 3" (7.5 cm) wide in slip-stitch patt from chart using larger needles.

NOTES

• In stockinette stitch, MC and CC always refer to a double strand of Tvinni Alpaca and Spinni held together. In slip-stitch panels, CC always refers to a single strand of Tvinni Alpaca. For the short accent stripes above and below the slip-stitch panels, use a double strand of either yarn, or one strand of each yarn held together, as desired.

• Instructions are not given for the placement of specific accent colors. For the garment shown, each slip-stitch panel uses different colors for its top and bottom stripes; feel free to experiment with any color combinations you find pleasing.

• Read about intarsia knitting on page 71. Work the MC and CC rectangles in stockinette intarsia, twisting the yarns at color change to avoid leaving holes.

• For the frame around the slip-stitch panels, use separate balls of MC and A above and below the patterned panels. When working the slip-stitch panel from chart, use a separate ball of CC for charted pattern area and use the MC from edge to edge across the entire square frame surrounding each panel. Twist the yarns at the color changes on either side of slip-stitch panels to avoid leaving holes.

• When working the chart patterns, slip stitches as if to purl with the unused color carried along the wrong side of the work. In other words, on the right-side rows slip as if to purl with yarn in back; on wrong-side rows slip as if to purl with yarn in front. The slipped strands should never float across the right side (public side) of the fabric.

• The color used for each pair of rows is indicated in brackets at the side of the chart.

• The slip-stitch pattern has a different row gauge from the surrounding stockinette areas. To introduce the necessary extra rows, chart rows worked with CC are worked back and forth over the stitches of the slip-stitch panel *only*, without working the surrounding MC stockinette background stitches.

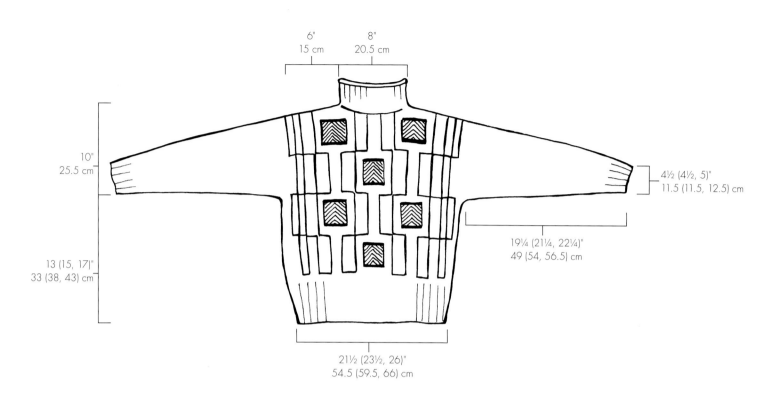

6"
15 cm
8"
20.5 cm
10"
25.5 cm
4½ (4½, 5)"
11.5 (11.5, 12.5) cm
19¼ (21¼, 22¼)"
49 (54, 56.5) cm
13 (15, 17)"
33 (38, 43) cm
21½ (23½, 26)"
54.5 (59.5, 66) cm

BACK

With MC and smaller 24" (60 cm) cir needle, CO 135 (147, 163) sts. Do not join into a rnd. *Set up rib:* (RS) K1 (selvedge st; knit every row), k0 (3, 3), p0 (3, 3), [k5, p3] 16 (16, 18) times, k5, p0 (3, 3), k0 (3, 3), k1 (selvedge st; knit every row). Knitting the first and last st of every row for selvedge sts, work in rib patt as established until piece measures 3 (5, 7)" (7.5 [12.5, 19] cm) from CO edge, ending with a RS row, and placing markers (pm) on either side of center 125 sts on last row—125 marked center sts; 5 (11, 19) sts at each side. Change to larger 24" (60 cm) cir needle. *Note:* From here until the armhole shaping, knit the first and last st of every row for selvedge sts and work sts on either side of marked center patt sts in established rib with MC.

INTARSIA PATTERNS

Prepare 7 bobbins or yarn butterflies of MC, and 6 bobbins of CC. *Set-up row:* (WS) Work 5 (11, 19) sts as established with MC, slip marker (sl m), p5 with MC, p5 with CC, [p9 with MC, p10 with CC] 2 times, p29 with MC, [p10 with CC, p9 with MC] 2 times, p5 with CC, p5 with MC, sl m, work rem 5 (11, 19) sts as established with MC.

Rows 1–9: Work 9 rows in established colors, working marked center 125 sts in St st intarsia, working sts at each side in rib patt with selvedge sts, and ending with a RS row.

Row 10: Work as established to 29 center MC sts, p5 with MC, join A, p19 with A, join separate bobbin of MC, p5 with MC, work as established to end.

Rows 11 and 12: Work 2 rows in patt and colors as established—3 rows of accent color stripe completed. Break off A.

Row 13: (RS) Work as established to 29 center sts, k5 with MC, drop MC to WS, join CC for slip-stitch panel (see Notes, page 66), k19 center sts with CC, turn, knit back across same 19 sts, drop CC to WS, turn, with MC and RS facing, work Row 1 of Slip-Stitch Panel chart (page 68) across center 19 sts, k5 with same ball of MC, work as established to end.

Row 14: Work as established to center 19 sts, work Row 2 of chart with MC across center 19 sts, work as established to end.

Row 15: Work as established to center 19 sts, drop MC to WS, with CC work Row 3 of chart across 19 center sts, turn, work Row 4 of chart across same 19 sts, drop CC to WS, turn, with MC and RS facing, work Row 5 of chart across center 19 sts, work as established to end.

MC: knit on RS

• MC: knit on WS

V MC: slip on both RS and WS

CC: knit on RS

• CC: knit on WS

V CC: slip on both RS and WS

Slip-stitch Panel

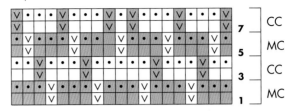

Row 16: Work as established to center 19 sts, work Row 6 of chart with MC across 19 sts, work as established to end.

Row 17: Work as established to center 19 sts, drop MC to WS, with CC work Row 7 of chart across 19 center sts, turn, work Row 8 of chart across same 19 sts, drop CC on WS, turn, with MC and RS facing, work Row 1 of chart across center 19 sts, work as established to end.

Row 18: Work as established to center 19 sts, work Row 2 of chart with MC across 19 sts, work as established to end.

Row 19: Work as established to center 19 sts, drop MC to WS, with CC work Row 3 of chart across 19 center sts, turn, work Row 4 of chart across same 19 sts, drop CC to WS, turn, with MC and RS facing, work Row 5 of chart across center 19 sts, work as established to end.

Row 20: Work as established to center 19 sts, work Row 6 of chart with MC across 19 sts, work as established to end.

Rows 21–32: Rep Rows 17–20 three more times.

Row 33: Work as established to center 19 sts, drop MC to WS, with CC work Row 7 of chart across 19 center sts, turn, work Row 8 of chart across same 19 sts, drop CC to WS, turn—Rows 1–8 of chart have been worked a total of 5 times; 40 chart rows completed, plus 2 garter st set-up rows with CC in Row 13. Break off CC. With RS facing, sl center 19 sts to right-hand needle without working any sts. With RS still facing, join new ball of MC, k5 with MC, work as established to end.

Row 34: Work as established to 29 center sts, p5 with MC, join A, p19 with A, p5 with MC, work as established to end.

Rows 35 and 36: Work 2 rows in patt and colors as established—3 rows of accent color stripe completed. Break off A.

Rows 37–47: Work 11 rows even in patt, working center

29 sts with MC only, and ending with a RS row. Break off MC and CC—piece measures about 5" (12.5 cm) from top of rib including set-up row, and about 8 (10, 12)" (20.5 [25.5, 30.5] cm) from CO edge.

Row 48: (WS) Prepare 7 bobbins or yarn butterflies of MC, and 6 bobbins or butterflies of CC. Set up second tier of rectangles and patterned panels as foll: Work 5 (11, 19) sts as established with MC, sl m, p5 with CC, p5 with MC, p9 with CC, p29 with MC, p10 with CC, p9 with MC, p10 with CC, p29 with MC, p9 with CC, p5 with MC, p5 with CC, sl m, work 5 (11, 19) sts as established with MC—two 29-st panels with MC in second tier.

Rows 49–57: Work 9 rows in patt and colors as established, ending with a RS row.

Row 58: Work in patt and colors as established to 29-st group of MC sts, *p5 with MC, join A, p19 with A, join separate bobbin of MC, p5 with MC,* work in established colors to next 29-st group of MC sts, rep from * to * using a different accent color for second group, work in patt and colors as established to end.

Rows 59 and 60: Work 2 rows in patt and colors as established—3 rows of accent color stripes completed. Break off both colors A.

Row 61: Work in patt and colors as established to first 19-st accent-color group, drop MC to WS, *join CC for slip-stitch panel, k19 with CC, turn, knit back across same 19 sts, drop CC to WS, turn, with MC and RS facing, work Row 1 of Slip-Stitch Panel chart across same 19 sts, k5 with same ball of MC,* work in established colors to next 19-st accent-color group, drop MC to WS, rep from * to * once more, work in patt and colors as established to end.

Row 62: Work in patt and colors as established, working Row 2 of chart with MC across each 19-st slip-stitch group.

Row 63: Work in patt and colors as established to first 19-st slip-stitch group, drop MC to WS, *with CC work Row 3 of chart across 19 sts, turn, work Row 4 of chart across same 19 sts, drop CC to WS, turn, with MC and RS facing, work Row 5 of chart across 19 sts,* work in established colors to next 19-st slip-stitch group, drop MC to WS, rep from * to * once more, work in patt and colors as established to end.

Row 64: Work in patt and colors as established, working Row 6 of chart with MC across each 19-st slip-stitch group.

Row 65: Work in patt and colors as established to first 19-st slip-stitch group, drop MC to WS, *with CC, work Row 7 of chart across 19 sts, turn, work Row 8 of chart across same 19 sts, drop CC to WS, turn, with MC and RS facing, work Row 1 of chart across 19 sts,* work in established colors to next 19-st slip-stitch group, drop MC to WS, rep from * to * once more, work in patt and colors as established to end.

Row 66: Work in patt and colors as established, working Row 2 of chart with MC across each 19-st slip-stitch group.

Row 67: Work in patt and colors as established to first 19-st slip-stitch group, drop MC to WS, *with CC work Row 3 of chart across 19 sts, turn, work Row 4 of chart across same 19 sts, drop CC to WS, turn, with MC and RS facing, work Row 5 of chart across 19 sts,* work in established colors to next 19-st slip-stitch group, drop MC to WS, rep from * to * once more, work in patt and colors as established to end.

Row 68: Work in patt and colors as established, working Row 6 of chart with MC across each 19-st slip-stitch group.

Rows 69–80: Rep Rows 65–68 three more times.

Row 81: Work in patt and colors as established to first 19-st slip-stitch group, drop MC to WS, *with CC work Row 7 of chart across 19 sts, turn, work Row 8 of chart across same 19 sts, drop CC on WS, turn, with RS facing, sl 19 sts to right-hand needle without working any sts, join new ball of MC, k5 with MC,* work in established colors to next 19-st slip-stitch group, drop MC to WS, rep from * to * once more, work in patt and colors as established to end. Break off CC.

Row 82: Work in patt and colors as established to first 19-st slip-stitch group, join A, p19 with A, work in established colors to next 19-st slip-stitch group, join different A, p19 with A, work in patt and colors as established to end.

Rows 83 and 84: Work 2 rows in patt and colors as established—3 rows of accent color stripes completed. Break off both colors A.

Rows 85–95: Work 11 rows even in patt, working both 29-st groups with MC only, and ending with a RS row—piece measures about 10" (25.5 cm) from top of rib, and about 13 (15, 17)" (33 [38, 43] cm) from CO edge.

Break off MC and CC. Prepare 7 bobbins or yarn butterflies of MC, and 6 bobbins or butterflies of CC. Work WS set-up row at beg of Intarsia Patterns (page 67) again to establish third tier of rectangles.

SHAPE ARMHOLES

Work Rows 1 and 2 from beg of Intarsia Patterns, and *at the same time* BO 5 (11, 19) sts at beg of each row—125 sts rem for all sizes. Work Rows 3–95 over rem 125 center sts, knitting the first and last st of every row to re-establish the selvedge sts—armholes measure about 10" (25.5 cm) for all sizes; piece measures about 23 (25, 27)" (58.5 [63.5, 68.5] cm) from CO edge. Place sts on holder.

FRONT

Work as for back until Row 78 above the armholes has been completed—armholes measure about 8¼" (21 cm) for all sizes, ending with a WS row—125 sts for all sizes.

SHAPE FRONT NECK

On the next RS row, work in patt to center 19 sts, place 19 sts on holder, join new ball of yarn if necessary, work in patt to end—53 sts at each side. Working each side separately, at each neck edge BO 5 sts once, then BO 3 sts once, then BO 2 sts 2 times, then BO 1 st 3 times—38 sts rem at each side. Work even until Row 95 has been completed. Place sts on holder.

SLEEVES

With MC and smaller 16" (40 cm) cir needle, CO 56 (56, 64) sts. Do not join into a rnd. *Set up rib:* (RS) K1 (selvedge st; knit every row), k2, [p3, k5] 6 (6, 7) times, p3, k1, k1 (selvedge st; knit every row). Knitting the first and last st

of every row for selvedge sts, work in rib as established until piece measures 1¾" (4.5 cm) from CO, ending with a WS row. Change to larger 16" (60 cm) cir needle and St st. Beg with the next RS row, inc 1 st at each end of needle inside selvedge sts every 0 (0, 6) rows 0 (0, 8) times, then every 4 rows 34 (34, 22) times, changing to 24" (60 cm) cir needle when necessary—124 sts for all sizes; piece measures about 16" (40.5 cm) from CO. Work even until piece measures 19¼ (21¼, 22¼)" (49 [54, 56.5] cm) from CO. BO all sts.

FINISHING
JOIN SHOULDERS

Place 38 sts each for front and back left shoulders on ends of larger 24" (60 cm) cir needle. Turn work carefully inside out, and with right sides touching, use the three-needle bind-off technique (see Glossary, page 140) and other larger cir needle to join left shoulders tog. Rep for right shoulder. Leave 49 sts at center back neck on holder.

NECKBAND

Place 49 held back neck sts on larger 16" (40 cm) cir needle and join MC with RS facing. Work across 49 back neck sts in St st, pick up and knit 63 sts along shaped front neck edge—112 sts. Pm and join for working in the rnd. *Set up rib:* K3, [p3, k5] 13 times, p3, k2—center 5 sts on both front and back should be k5. Work even in rib as established until neckband measures 2¾" (7 cm) from pick-up rnd or desired length.

Neckband facing: Change to smaller 16" (40 cm) cir needle and join A (2 strands of #24s orange heather for sweater shown). Knit 1 rnd, then purl 1 rnd for turning ridge. Work even in St st for 3 rnds. Break off 1 strand of A, and cont in St st with single strand until neckband measures 2¾" (7 cm) from turning ridge. BO all sts loosely.

With yarn threaded on a tapestry needle, sew sleeves into armholes. Sew sleeve and side seams. Fold neckband facing to the inside along turning ridge and sew in place. Weave in loose ends. Carefully steam-press sweater under a damp cloth.

Intarsia is a method of working isolated areas of color. Separate balls of yarn are used for each section, or block, of color. The most important thing to remember when knitting intarsia is that the yarns need to be twisted around each other at the color changes. Otherwise, there will be gaps (holes) between the different colors of knitting.

KNITTING INTARSIA

To practice intarsia knitting, you will need needles and one ball each of a dark- and light-colored yarn.

With the dark yarn, cast on 4 stitches. With the light yarn, cast on 4 more stitches onto the same needle (Figure 1). Turn the work around to work the first wrong-side row. Work in stockinette stitch as follows:

Wrong-side (purl) rows: With the light yarn, purl the 4 light stitches, then drop the light yarn to front (purl side) of the work. Pick up the dark yarn from underneath the light yarn (Figure 2), then use it to purl the 4 dark stitches.

Right-side (knit) rows: With the dark yarn, knit the 4 dark stitches, then drop the dark yarn to the back (purl side) of the work. Bring the light yarn over the dark yarn (Figure 3), then knit the next 4 stitches with the light yarn.

Repeat these two rows, always dropping the old color to the wrong (purl) side of the work and always picking up the new color from under the old. Pull gently on the new color before knitting the first stitch to close the gap between the two colors.

If a pattern calls for many blocks of color in the same row, wind a separate butterfly of yarn for each section to prevent the yarns from tangling with each other. To make a butterfly, wind the yarn into a figure-eight around your thumb and little finger the desired number of times. To finish, wind the yarn around the center of the bundle a couple of times, then secure the tail on one of these center wraps (Figure 4). Pull the working end from the center (shown with an arrow) as needed.

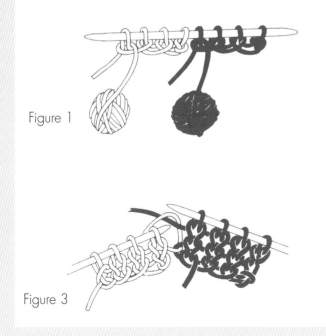

Figure 1

Figure 3

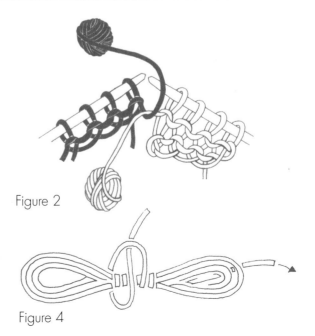

Figure 2

Figure 4

Inspired by mud-dyed cotton fabrics produced in the Bamana region of Mali, the body of this intricately patterned pullover is knitted in the round from the hemmed lower edge to the shoulders; extra stitches are cast on for armhole steeks that allow for shaping without interrupting the circular knitting rhythm. The steek stitches are secured, then the armholes and front neck are cut open to accommodate the neckband and sleeves—also worked in the round from the hemmed lower edge to the armhole. Stockinette-stitch facings conceal the raw edges of the cut armholes. The neck is finished with a narrow rolled edge followed by a double-thick neckband.

MATERIALS

SIZES 42½ (47, 52)" (108 [119.5, 132] cm finished chest/bust circumference. Shown in size 47" (119.5 cm).

YARN About 275 (300, 325) g of color A and 225 (250, 275) g of color B of fingering-weight (CYCA Super Fine #1) yarn.

Shown here: Isager Tvinni (100% merino lambswool; 558 yd [510 m]/100 g): #30 black (A), 3 (3, 4) skeins; #38s mustard yellow heather (B), 3 (3, 3) skeins.

NEEDLES U.S. sizes 2 and 4 (3 and 3.5 mm): 16" (40 cm) circular (cir), 32" (80 cm) cir, and set of 4 or 5 double-pointed (dpn). Adjust needle size if necessary to obtain the correct gauge.

NOTIONS A few yards (meters) of waste yarn; stitch markers (m); stitch holders; tapestry needle; sharp-point sewing needle or sewing machine; contrasting basting thread for steeks; matching sewing thread for steeks.

GAUGE 30½ sts and 33½ rnds = 4" (10 cm) in two-color stranded St st from charts using larger needle; 30 sts and 37 rnds = 4" (10 cm) in squares patt for shoulder area and sleeves using larger needles.

NOTES

- Read about stranded two-color knitting on page 96. For this project, color B is the dominant color. To create a uniform fabric throughout, notice how you handle the yarns in order to make B the dominant color, and always use the yarns in the same manner when working in the round. Experiment with your gauge swatch until you have achieved the desired effect.

- The design of the center back and front panels is deliberately not mirror-image symmetrical at both sides of the panel.

- For the Side chart, work the stitches outlined in red 0 (1, 2) times according to your size. This means that for the smallest size you will just skip over these stitches without working them at all. For the middle size, you will work the chart as it appears, and for the largest size, you will work the stitches outlined in red two times before working to the end of the chart.

BODY

With A and smaller 32" (80 cm) cir needle, CO 318 (352, 388) sts. Place marker (pm), and join for working in the rnd, being careful not to twist sts. Work even in St st for 1¼" (3.2 cm). Mark the last rnd completed in several places with waste yarn to indicate fold line for hem. Change to larger 32" (80 cm) cir needle, and knit 1 rnd, inc 6 (8, 8) sts evenly spaced—324 (360, 396) sts. Knit 1 more rnd—2 rnds completed with A on larger needle.

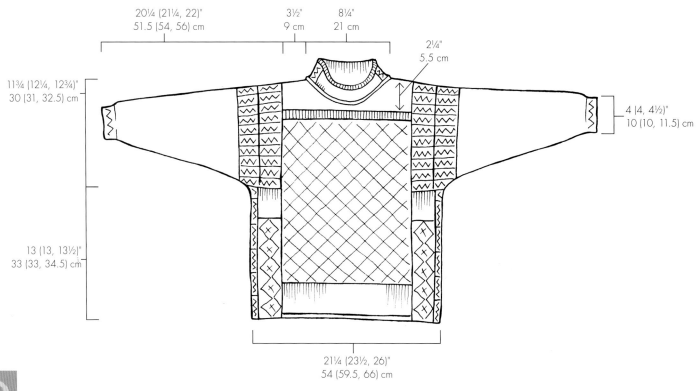

20¼ (21¼, 22)"
51.5 (54, 56) cm

3½"
9 cm

8¼"
21 cm

2¼"
5.5 cm

11¾ (12¼, 12¾)"
30 (31, 32.5) cm

4 (4, 4½)"
10 (10, 11.5) cm

13 (13, 13½)"
33 (33, 34.5) cm

21¼ (23½, 26)"
54 (59.5, 66) cm

work 0 (1, 2) times

147

141

131

121

111

101

91

81

71

61

51

41

31

21

11

1

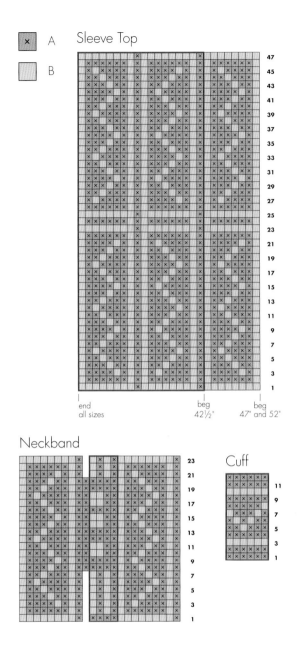

A ✕

B

Sleeve Top

(chart with round numbers on right: 47, 45, 43, 41, 39, 37, 35, 33, 31, 29, 27, 25, 23, 21, 19, 17, 15, 13, 11, 9, 7, 5, 3, 1)

end
all sizes | beg 42½" | beg 47" and 52"

Neckband

(chart with round numbers: 23, 21, 19, 17, 15, 13, 11, 9, 7, 5, 3, 1)

Cuff

(chart with round numbers: 11, 9, 7, 5, 3, 1)

Establish Side charts and work squares and vertical stripes for lower edge as foll:

Rnd 1: *[K2 with A, k2 with B] 28 times, k3 with A, pm, work 47 (65, 83) sts according to Rnd 1 of Side chart (page 75; see Notes, page 74), pm; rep from * once more—2 marked groups of 115 sts for center front and back panels, 2 marked groups of 47 (65, 83) sts worked according to Side chart; rnd begins at start of center back panel.

Rnd 2: *Work sts of center panel in colors as they appear, work Rnd 2 of chart over side panel sts; rep from * once more.

Rnds 3 and 4: *Work all sts of center panel with A only, work Rnd 3 and 4 of chart over side panel sts; rep from * once more.

Rnd 5: *K1 with A, k113 with B, k1 with A, work Rnd 5 of chart over side panel sts; rep from * once more.

Rnd 6: *[K1 with A, k1 with B] 57 times, k1 with A, work Rnd 6 of chart over side panel sts; rep from * once more.

Rnds 7–38: Work sts of both center panels in colors as they appear, work Rnds 7–38 of chart over side panel sts.

Rnd 39: *K1 with A, k113 with B, k1 with A, work Rnd 39 of chart over side panel sts; rep from * once more—piece measures about 5" (12.5 cm) from marked fold line, or 6¼" (16 cm) from CO, after completing Rnd 39.

SET UP CENTER CHARTS

*Work 114 sts according to Rnd 1 of Center chart (page 76) over center panel sts, dec 1 st in middle of center panel, work Rnd 40 of Side chart over side panel sts; rep from * once more—322 (358, 394) sts: 2 marked groups of 114 sts for center panels, 2 marked groups of 47 (65, 83) sts for side panels. Cont in patts as established until Rnd 106 (106, 110) of Side chart and Rnd 67 (67, 71) of Center chart have been completed—piece measures about 13 (13, 13½)" (33 [33, 34.5] cm) from marked fold line.

SHAPE ARMHOLES

*Work in patt across 114 center panel sts, BO next 47 (65, 83) sts for side panel; rep from * once more—2 groups of 114 sts rem. Rejoin for working in the rnd. Next rnd: *Work in patt over 114 center panel sts, pm, use backward loop method (see Glossary, page 139) to CO 4 sts with A over bind-off gap of previous rnd, pm; rep from * once more—236 sts: 2 groups of 114 sts for center front and back panels, 4 marked steek sts at each side. Work even in patt, working steek sts in St st with A, until Rnd 147 of Center chart has been completed—piece measures about 22½" (57 cm) from marked fold line; armholes measure about 9½ (9½, 9)" (24 [24, 23] cm). Work vertical stripes patt across center panels as foll:

Rnd 1: *K1 with A, knit to last st of center panel with B, and at the same time inc 1 st middle of panel, k1 with A, work 4 steek sts; rep from * once more—238 sts: 2 groups of 115 sts for center front and back panels, 4 marked steek sts at each side.

Rnds 2–7: *[K1 with A, k1 with B] 57 times, k1 with A, work 4 steek sts; rep from * once more.

Rnd 8: *K1 with A, k113 with B, k1 with A, work 4 steek

sts; rep from * once more—piece measures about 23½" (59.5 cm) from marked fold line; armholes measure about 10½ (10½, 10)" (26.5 [26.5, 25.5] cm).

Work squares patt for shoulder area as foll:

Rnds 1 and 2: Knit all sts with A.

Rnds 3 and 4: *[K2 with A, k2 with B] 28 times, k3 with A, work 4 steek sts; rep from * once more.

Rep Rnds 1–4 of squares patt 2 (3, 4) more times, then work Rnds 1 and 2 once more—14 (18, 22) rnds completed of squares patt; piece measures about 24¾ (25¼, 26¼)" (63 [64, 66.5] cm) from marked fold line; armholes measure about 11¾ (12¼, 12¾)" (30 [31, 32.5] cm). Place sts on separate holders for front and back, dividing the steek sts evenly between them—119 sts on each holder; 2 steek sts at each side of both front and back.

SLEEVES

With A and smaller dpn, CO 60 (60, 66) sts. Pm, and join for working in the rnd, being careful not to twist sts. *Next rnd:* *K1 with A, k1 with B; rep from * to end. Rep this row for vertical stripes until piece measures 2" (5 cm) from CO. Mark the last rnd completed in several places with waste yarn to indicate fold line for hem. Change to larger dpn. Work even in established vertical stripes until piece measures ½" (1.3 cm) from marked fold line, or 2½" (6.5 cm) from CO. Work Rnds 1–12 of Cuff chart, inc 12 (12, 14) sts evenly in Rnd 12—72 (72, 80) sts; piece measures about 2" (5 cm) from marked fold line. Work squares patt for sleeves as foll:

Rnds 1 and 2: K1 with A (edge st, work in A throughout), *k2 with A, k2 with B; rep from * to last 3 sts, k2 with A, k1 with A (edge st, work in A throughout).

Rnds 3 and 4: Knit all sts with A.

Rep Rnds 1–4 for patt, and *at the same time,* beg with the next Rnd 1, inc 1 st at each side inside edge sts every other rnd 49 (51, 42) times, working inc'd sts into squares patt, and changing to larger cir needle as necessary to accommodate the number of sts—170 (174, 164) sts. Inc 1 st at each side inside edge sts every 3rd rnd 4 (5, 14) times—178 (184, 192) sts. Work 2 (3, 2) rnds even to end with Rnd 4 of squares patt—piece measures about 14½ (15½, 16¼)" (37 [39.5, 41.5] cm) from marked fold line.

SET UP SLEEVE TOP CHART

K2 (1, 2) with A, [k1 with B, k1 with A] 3 (3, 0) times, work center 162 (170, 188) sts according to Rnd 1 of Sleeve Top chart, beg and ending where indicated for your size, [k1 with A, k1 with B] 3 (3, 0) times, k2 (1, 2) with A.

Cont in patt, working sts at each side of chart in vertical stripes as established, until Rnd 47 of Sleeve Top chart has been completed—piece measures about 20¼ (21¼, 22)" (51.5 [54, 56] cm) from marked fold line. With A only, work in solid-color St st for ⅝" (1.5 cm) for armhole facing. Loosely BO all sts.

FINISHING

CUT FRONT NECK OPENING

Place center 63 sts at center back and front on holders, leaving rem 28 sts at each side on separate holders for shoulders. Measure down 2¼" (5.5 cm) from top of piece at center front. Baste the outline of a rounded front neck opening, starting at one edge of the center sts, down to the center front, and back up to the other edge of the center sts. With sewing machine or by hand, sew two lines of small straight stitches along the front basting line. Cut out front neck opening about ¼" (6 mm) inside the basting line to leave a small seam allowance. Back neckline is not shaped; leave 63 back neck sts on holder.

CUT ARMHOLES

Baste a line of contrasting thread along the center of each set of 4 steek sts. With sewing machine or by hand, sew a line of small straight stitches one stitch away on both sides of the basting line. Sew over the same line of stitching again. Carefully cut open the armholes along the basting line.

CUT SLEEVE STEEKS

Measure down 3 (4¼, 5½)" (7.5 [11, 14] cm) from BO edge of sleeve along center of underarm and mark with waste yarn. Baste a line of contrasting thread 3 (4¼, 5½)" (7.5 [11, 14] cm) long along the line between the edge sts to the marked position. With sewing machine or by hand, sew a line of small straight stitches one stitch away on each side of the basting line and across the bottom of the steek. Sew over the same line of stitching again. Carefully cut open the sleeve steeks along the basting line from BO edge to marked position.

JOIN SHOULDERS

Place about 28 sts each for front and back left shoulder on ends of larger cir needle. *Note:* 1 or 2 sts at each cut edge may have been eliminated by the armhole steeks, so you may have fewer shoulder sts available. Turn work carefully inside out, and with right sides touching, use the three-needle bind-off technique (see Glossary, page 140) and single larger dpn to join left shoulders tog. Repeat for right shoulder.

SET IN SLEEVES

With yarn threaded on a tapestry needle and using a mattress st (see Glossary, page 141), sew the last patt rnd at top of sleeve (just below the St st armhole facing) to cut edge of armhole one st inside the lines of stitching. On WS, smooth the armhole facing over the cut edge and sew in place with yarn threaded on a tapestry needle.

NECKBAND

Place 63 held back neck sts on larger 16" (40 cm) cir needle, and with RS facing join B to beg of sts. Knit across 63 back neck sts, pm, pick up and knit 75 sts along cut front neck opening, picking up just below the stitching lines—138 sts; rnd starts at beg of back neck sts. Pm and join for working in the rnd. Knit 6 rnds.

Neckband welt: With smaller 16" (40 cm) cir needle and WS facing, pick up the purl bumps of 138 sts at the base of the St st rnds just worked; do not pick up and knit these sts, simply slip the needle into the purl bumps along the first rnd. Fold 6 rnds of St st in half with wrong sides touching to bring both needles parallel. With other end of larger cir needle, *k2tog, knitting the first st on each needle tog; rep from * to end—138 sts. Change to A and knit 1 rnd, dec 1 st each at center front and back—136 sts rem; 62 front sts, 74 back sts.

SET UP NECKBAND CHART

From Rnd 1 of chart, work 9 sts before repeat box of Neckband chart once, work 4-st rep 11 times across front neck, work 9 sts after rep box once, sl m, work 9 sts before repeat box once, work 4-st rep 14 times across back neck, work 9 sts after rep box once. Work Rnds 2–7 of chart. On Rnd 8, inc 1 st after last rep on both front and back as shown on chart—138 sts: 63 front sts, 75 back sts. Work even until Rnd 20 of chart has been completed. On Rnd 21, dec 1 st after last rep on both front and back as shown—136 sts: 62 front sts, 74 back sts. Cont until Rnd 23 has been completed. Work all neckband sts in vertical stripes (k1 with A, k1 with B) as established for 4 rnds—neckband measures about 3¼" (8.5 cm) from neckband welt. Mark the last rnd completed in several places with waste yarn to indicate fold line for neckband.

Neckband facing: Change to smaller 16" (40 cm) cir needle, and work even in vertical stripes until neckband facing measures 3¼" (8.5 cm) from marked fold line. BO all sts loosely.

Fold lower body and sleeve hems to the inside along marked fold lines. With yarn threaded on a tapestry needle, sew hems in place. Fold neckband to inside along fold line and sew in place to cover cut edge of neck opening. Weave in loose ends. Carefully steam-press sweater under a damp cloth.

Diamond and zigzag patterns in a Zairian cloth that was
woven, embroidered, and plant-dyed have inspired the
allover Fair Isle patterning on this cropped pullover.
The sweater is knitted in the round in a single piece
from cuff to cuff, with steeks along the lower body and
neck edges. The knitted stitches are secured along the
steeks, then the piece is cut open and the raw edges are
concealed with knitted facings. The dolman shaping on
the sleeves provides a comfortable fit and allows the
zigzag pattern of the upper sleeves to flow seamlessly
into the diamond pattern on the front and back.

MATERIALS

SIZES 37½ (44, 50½)" (95 (112, 128.5] cm) finished chest/bust circumference. Shown in size 44" (112 cm).

YARN About 200 (200, 300) g each of two colors of fingering-weight (CYCA Super Fine #1) yarn.

Shown here: Isager Tvinni (100% merino lambswool; 558 yd [510 m]/100 g): #24s orange heather (A), and #35s yellow heather (B), 2 (2, 3) skeins each. Also shown in #47 charcoal (A) and #7s medium brown heather (B).

NEEDLES U.S. sizes 2 and 4 (3 and 3.5 mm): 16" (40 cm) and 24" (60 cm) circular (cir) and set of 4 or 5 double-pointed (dpn). Adjust needle size if necessary to obtain the correct gauge.

NOTIONS Stitch markers (m); tapestry needle; removable marker or safety pin; sharp-point sewing needle or sewing machine; contrasting basting thread for steeks; matching sewing thread for steeks.

GAUGE 28 sts and 32 rows = 4" (10 cm) in two-color stranded St st from charts using larger needles.

NOTES

- Read about stranded two-color knitting on page 96. For this project, color B is the dominant color. To create a uniform fabric throughout, notice how you handle the yarns in order to make B the dominant color, and always use the yarns in the same manner when working in the round or knitting right-side rows. When purling wrong-side rows, reverse the positions of the two yarns in order to keep color B dominant. Experiment with your gauge swatch until you have achieved the desired effect.

- As an alternative to working a separate gauge swatch, you can steam-press the piece after working 4–6" (10–15 cm) on larger needles for the first sleeve cuff, then measure it over the two-color pattern area to check your gauge. Be prepared to change needle size, if necessary, to obtain the correct gauge.

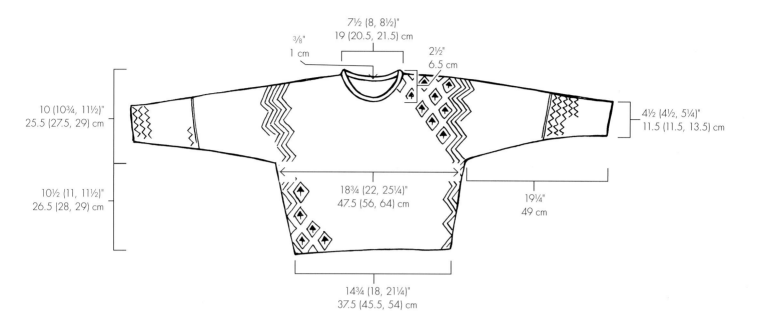

Measurements on schematic:

7½ (8, 8½)"
19 (20.5, 21.5) cm

3⁄8"
1 cm

2½"
6.5 cm

10 (10¾, 11½)"
25.5 (27.5, 29) cm

4½ (4½, 5¼)"
11.5 (11.5, 13.5) cm

10½ (11, 11½)"
26.5 (28, 29) cm

18¾ (22, 25¼)"
47.5 (56, 64) cm

19¼"
49 cm

14¾ (18, 21¼)"
37.5 (45.5, 54) cm

LEFT SIDE

LEFT SLEEVE

With B and smaller dpn, CO 60 (60, 68) sts. Place marker (pm) and join for working in the rnd, being careful not to twist sts. Work St st (knit every rnd) for sleeve facing until piece measures ¾" (2 cm) from beg, inc 4 (4, 6) sts evenly spaced on last rnd—64 (64, 74) sts. Change to larger dpn. Join A and work Rnds 1–4 of Left Sleeve Triangles chart (see page 84), using B as the dominant color (see Notes), and beg and ending where indicated for your size. *Inc rnd:* Cont in patt, work first st, M1 (see Glossary, page 140), work in patt to last st, M1, work last st—2 sts inc'd. Work 2 rnds even in patt. *Note:* As sleeve increases, change to larger size cir needle when there are too many sts to fit comfortably on dpn. Cont patt from chart as established, rep the shaping of the last 3 rnds 15 more times, working inc'd sts into patt, and ending with Rnd 4 of chart—96 (96, 106) sts; 52 rnds completed from chart; piece measures about 6½" (16.5 cm) from beg of patt, and 7¼" (18.5 cm) from CO. *Next rnd:* Knit 1 rnd with B, inc 1 st at each end of rnd as before—98 (98, 108) sts. Knit 1 rnd A, then knit 1 rnd B. Work Rnd 1 of Left Sleeve Zigzag chart, inc 1 st at each end of rnd as before, and beg and ending where indicated for your size—100 (100, 110) sts. Work 2 rnds even. Cont patt from chart as established, rep the shaping of the last 3 rnds 20 (25, 25) more times, working inc'd sts into patt, and ending with Rnd 3 (8, 8) of chart—140 (150, 160) sts; 63 (78, 78) rnds of zigzags completed; piece measures about 14¾" (16½, 16½)" (37.5 [42, 42] cm) from beg of color work patt. Work even in patt from chart for 36 (21, 21) rnds, ending with Rnd 9 of chart. *Next rnd:* (Rnd 10 of chart) Inc 1 st at beg of rnd *only*—141 (151, 161) sts; sleeve measures about 19¼" (49 cm) from beg of color work patt, not counting ¾" (2 cm) for sleeve facing.

LEFT SIDE BODY

Change to larger 24" (60 cm) cir and work back and forth in rows (see Notes for how to maintain dominant color) as foll: Using the knitted method (see Glossary, page 139), CO 9 (9, 10) sts at beg of the next 14 rows, working new sts into zigzag patt—267 (277, 301) sts. CO 10 (14, 11) sts at beg of the foll 2 rows, ending with Row 6 of chart—287 (305, 323) sts; piece measures 2" (5 cm) from beg of side shaping. Pm after the first 2 sts and before the last 2 sts. When the piece is rejoined for working in the rnd, the

Left Sleeve Triangles

Right Sleeve Triangles

Left Sleeve Zigzag

Right Side Zigzag

Arrowheads

×	orange (A)
	yellow (B)
	pattern repeat

4 sts between these markers will be the steek sts for the lower opening. Work the 4 steek sts in a solid color, 1 × 1 check patt, or stripes, as you prefer in order to distinguish them from the patt sts.

CENTER BODY

Change to Arrowheads chart; rnd begins at lower edge of back, in the center of the 4 steek sts. Establish patt from Rnd 1 of Arrowheads chart over center 283 (301, 319) sts according to your size as foll: Work 2 steek sts, work 6 (15, 2) sts before first patt rep of chart once, work first 22-st patt rep 6 (6, 7) times, work center 7 sts once, work second 22-st patt rep 6 (6, 7) times, work 6 (15, 2) sts after second patt rep once, work rem 2 steek sts. Cont in patt until Rnd 26 has been completed, then rep entire 26-rnd chart 3 (4, 5) more times, then work Rnds 1–14 once more—118 (144, 170) rnds of arrowhead patt completed; piece measures about 14¾ (18, 21¼)" (37.5 [45.5, 54] cm) from end of side shaping, and 16¾ (20, 23¼)" (42.5 [51, 59] cm) from end of left sleeve.

RIGHT SIDE
RIGHT SIDE BODY

Change to Right Side Zigzag chart, beg and end according to your size. Cont to work 2 steek sts at each end of rnd, work Rnd 1 over center 283 (301, 319) sts to establish patt placement, beg and ending as indicated for your size. Working back and forth in rows, BO 10 (14, 11) sts at the beg of the next 2 rows, then BO 9 (9, 10) sts at beg of the foll 14 rows, ending with RS Row 7 of chart—141 (151,

Peter Wath

161) sts rem; piece measures about 2" (5 cm) from beg of right side shaping, and 18¾ (22, 25¼)" (47.5 [56, 64] cm) from end of left sleeve. Work WS Row 8 of chart, dec 1 st at end of row *only*—140 (150, 160) sts rem.

RIGHT SLEEVE

Pm and rejoin for working in the rnd. Cont even in zigzag patt for 34 (19, 19) rnds. *Dec rnd:* Work first st, ssk, work in patt to last 3 sts, k2tog, work last st—2 sts dec'd. Work 2 rnds even. Cont in patt from chart as established, rep the shaping of the last 3 rnds 20 (25, 25) more times, ending with Rnd 5 of Right Side Zigzag chart—98 (98, 108) sts rem; 97 rnds completed from beg of sleeve; sleeve measures about 12¼" (31 cm) from end of side shaping. *Note:* As sleeve decreases, change to larger size 16" (40 cm) cir needle or dpn as necessary. *Next rnd:* Knit 1 rnd with B, dec 1 st at each end of rnd as before—96 (96, 106) sts rem. Knit 1 rnd A, then knit 1 rnd B. Change to Right Sleeve Triangles chart, and work Rnd 1, dec 1 st at each end of rnd as before—94 (94, 104) sts rem. Work 2 rnds even. Cont in patt from chart, rep the shaping of the last 3 rnds 15 more times, ending with Rnd 8 of chart—64 (64, 74) sts rem. Work 4 rnds even, ending with Rnd 4 of chart—sleeve measures about 19¼" (49 cm) from end of side shaping. Break off A and change to smaller dpn. Knit 1 rnd, dec 4 (4, 6) sts evenly spaced—60 (60, 68) sts rem. Cont in St st until piece measures ¾" (2 cm) from last two-color patt rnd. BO all sts.

FINISHING

Carefully steam-press sweater under a damp cloth.

CUT STEEK

Baste a line of contrasting thread along the center of the 4-st steek at lower edge of sweater. With sewing machine or by hand, sew a line of small straight stitches one stitch away on each side of the basting line. Sew over the same two lines of stitching again. Carefully cut open the lower edge along the basting line.

CUT NECK OPENING

Mark the exact center of the shoulder line for center of neck opening. Measure 3¾ (4, 4¼)" (9.5 [10, 11] cm) on each side of center marker along shoulder line. Measure down 2½" (6.5 cm) at center front and ⅜" (1 cm) down at center back. Baste the outline of a rounded neck opening. Sew two lines of small straight stitches along the basting

line. Cut out the neck opening about ¼" (6 mm) inside the basting line to leave a small seam allowance.

NECKBAND

With smaller 16" (40 cm) cir needle, RS facing, and either A or B as preferred, pick up and knit about 94 (100, 108) sts around neck opening, picking up just below the stitching lines. Pm and join for working in the rnd. Knit every rnd until neckband measures ½" (1.3 cm) from pick-up. Purl 1 rnd for fold line, then knit ½" (1.3 cm) more for

facing. BO all sts. Fold band to inside along fold line and sew facing to WS to enclose cut neck edge. With smaller 16" (40 cm) cir needle, RS facing, and same color, pick up and knit 1 st in each purl bump of fold line. Pm and join for working in the rnd. Knit 6 rnds. BO all sts, allowing edging to roll to the outside.

SIDE SEAMS

With yarn threaded on a tapestry needle and using the mattress st (see Glossary, page 141), sew side seams.

LOWER EDGING

With smaller 24" (60-cm) cir needle, RS facing, and A or B as preferred, pick up and knit 190 (234, 276) sts along lower edge of sweater. Pm and join for working in the rnd. Knit every rnd until lower edging measures ¾" (2 cm) from pick-up rnd. BO all sts. Fold lower edging to WS along pick-up rnd. With yarn threaded on a tapestry needle, sew lower edging in place.

Weave in loose ends. Steam-press all edges and seams.

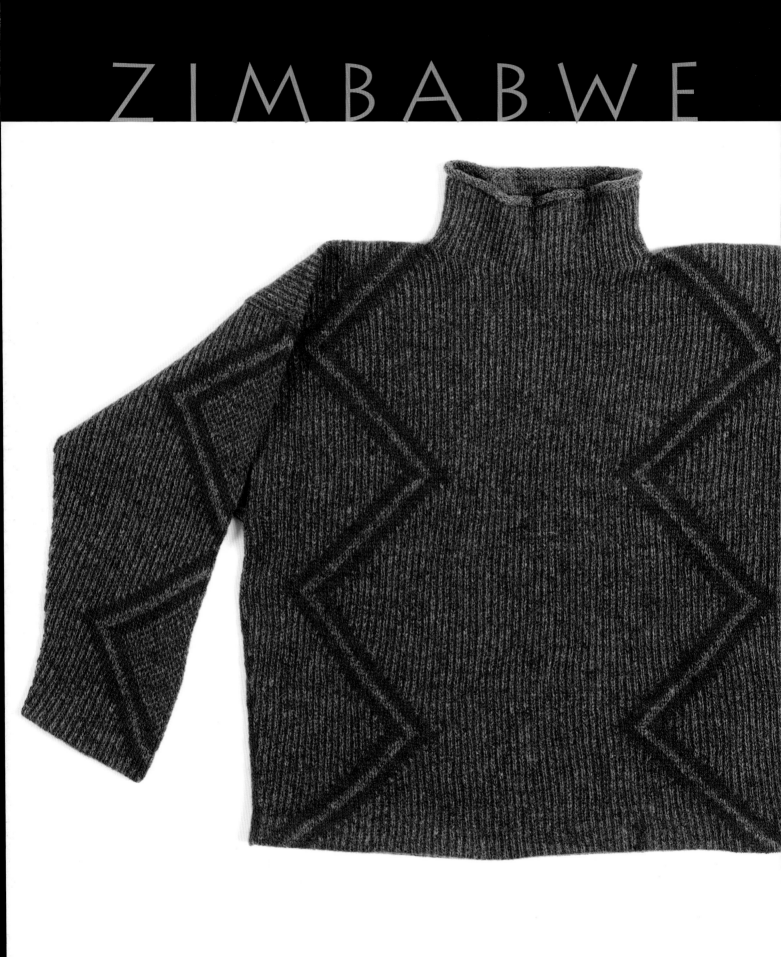

Handmade baskets are an important part of African craft. The narrow stripes and zigzag patterns on this sweater echo the interaction of two colors of reed woven into a basket purchased at a roadside stand near the Zimbabwean village of Bulawayo. The tapered body of the sweater is worked in the round from the hemmed lower edge to the shoulders, with extra stitches added along the way for armhole steeks, as for Mali on page 72. The sleeves are also worked in the round, from the hemmed cuffs to the armholes, and the gentle curve of the front neck is cut and sewn. Stockinette-stitch facings conceal the raw edges of the armholes and neck. Finished with a tiny rolled edge, the stand-up collar carefully maintains the stitch-for-stitch color pattern of the front and back.

MATERIALS

SIZES 36 (39, 42, 45, 49½)" (91.5 [99, 106.5, 114.5, 125.5] cm) finished chest/bust circumference. Shown in size 42" (106.5 cm).

YARN About 150 (175, 200, 225, 250) g each of two colors of fingering-weight (CYCA Super Fine #1) yarn.

Shown here: Isager Tvinni (100% merino lambswool; 558 yd [510 m]/100 g): #47 dark blue-gray (A), 2 (2, 2, 3, 3) skeins

Isager Highland (100% pure new wool; 612 yd [560 m]/100 g): #4 damask (rose heather; B), 2 (2, 2, 3, 3) skeins.

Also shown in Tvinni #47 charcoal (A) and #7s medium gray heather (B) on page 89.

NEEDLES U.S. sizes 2 and 4 (3 and 3.5 mm): 16" (40 cm) and 32" (80 cm) circular (cir), and set of 4 or 5 double-pointed (dpn). Adjust needle size if necessary to obtain the correct gauge.

NOTIONS Stitch markers (m); tapestry needle; removable markers or safety pins; sharp-point sewing needle or sewing machine; contrasting basting thread for steeks; matching sewing thread for steeks.

GAUGE 32 sts and 30 rnds = 4" (10 cm) in stranded two-color St st using larger needles, and alternating 1 st A with 1 st B, working colors as they appear on foll rnds.

NOTES

- Read about stranded two-color knitting on page 96. For this project, color B is the dominant color. To create a uniform fabric throughout, notice how you handle the yarns in order to make B the dominant color, and always use the yarns in the same manner when working in the round or knitting right-side rows. When purling wrong-side rows, reverse the positions of the two yarns in order to keep color B dominant. Experiment with your gauge swatch until you have achieved the desired effect.

- As an alternative to working a separate gauge swatch, begin by working a sleeve. You can steam-press the piece after working 6 to 8" (15 to 20 cm) on larger needles, then measure it over the two-color pattern area to check your gauge. Be prepared to change needle size, if necessary, to obtain the correct gauge.

- Cast on loosely for the lower edge of body and sleeve cuffs so the hemmed facings can stretch to accommodate the beginning of the body and sleeve shaping.

BODY

With B and smaller 32" (80 cm) cir needle, CO 256 (272, 288, 304, 332) sts. Place marker (pm), and join for working in the rnd, being careful not to twist sts. Work even in St st for 1¼" (3.2 cm), pm after the 128th (136th, 144th, 152nd, 166th) st in last rnd to indicate other side "seam"—2 marked sections; 128 (136, 144, 152, 166) sts each for front and back. Change to larger 32" (80 cm) cir needle. Set up edge sts and patt from charts as foll: *K1 with A (edge st; work in A throughout), pm, work Chart 1 for your size over 42 (42, 46, 46, 50) sts, pm, work center

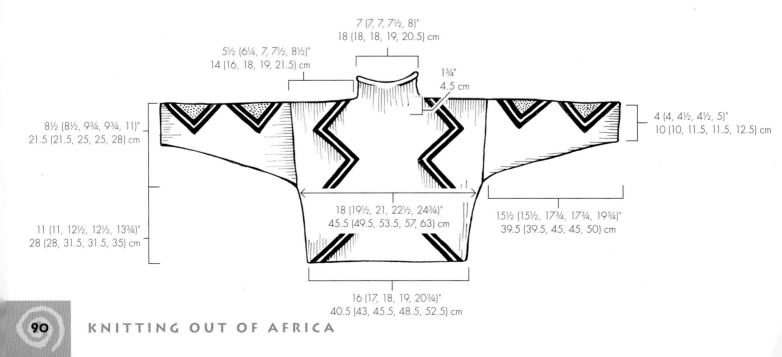

7 (7, 7, 7½, 8)"
18 (18, 18, 19, 20.5) cm

5½ (6¼, 7, 7½, 8½)"
14 (16, 18, 19, 21.5) cm

1¾"
4.5 cm

8½ (8½, 9¾, 9¾, 11)"
21.5 (21.5, 25, 25, 28) cm

4 (4, 4½, 4½, 5)"
10 (10, 11.5, 11.5, 12.5) cm

18 (19½, 21, 22½, 24¾)"
45.5 (49.5, 53.5, 57, 63) cm

15½ (15½, 17¾, 17¾, 19¾)"
39.5 (39.5, 45, 45, 50) cm

11 (11, 12½, 12½, 13¾)"
28 (28, 31.5, 31.5, 35) cm

16 (17, 18, 19, 20¾)"
40.5 (43, 45.5, 48.5, 52.5) cm

42 (50, 50, 58, 64) sts as [k1 with B, k1 with A] 21 (25, 25, 29, 32) times, pm, work Chart 2 (see page 93) for your size over 42 (42, 46, 46, 50) sts, pm, k1 with A (edge st; work in A throughout); rep from * once more. Cont in patt from charts, working vertical stripes of A and B as established, until Rnd 5 of charts has been completed.

SHAPE SIDES

Beg on the next rnd, inc 1 st at each side of both front and back, working incs inside edge sts, working inc'd sts into alternating vertical stripes patt, and maintaining edge sts in A throughout—4 sts inc'd. Cont in established patt and work 4 rnds even. Cont in patt, rep the shaping of the last 5 rnds 6 (8, 10, 12, 14) more times, then work

 A

B

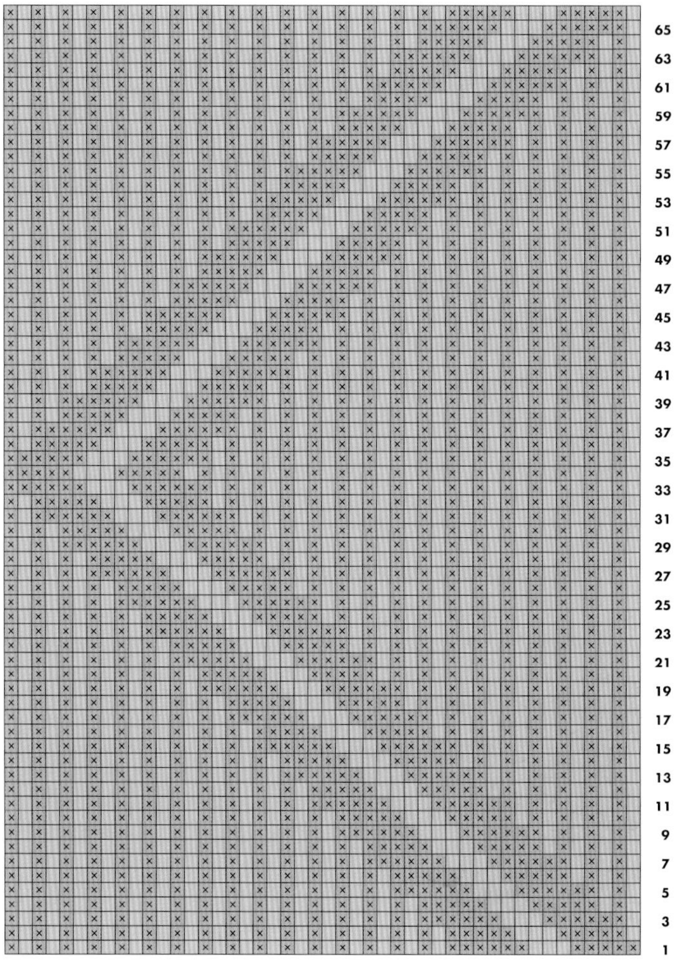

Chart 1 Size 49½"

Chart 1 Sizes 42" and 45"

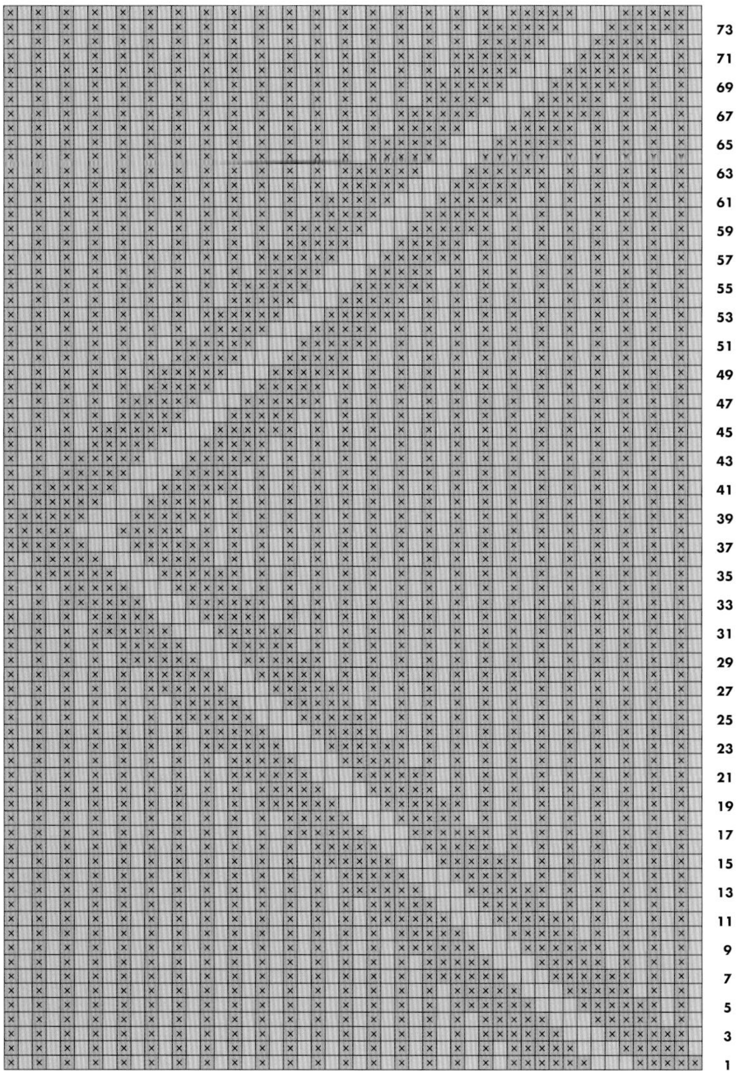

Chart 1 Sizes 36" and 39"

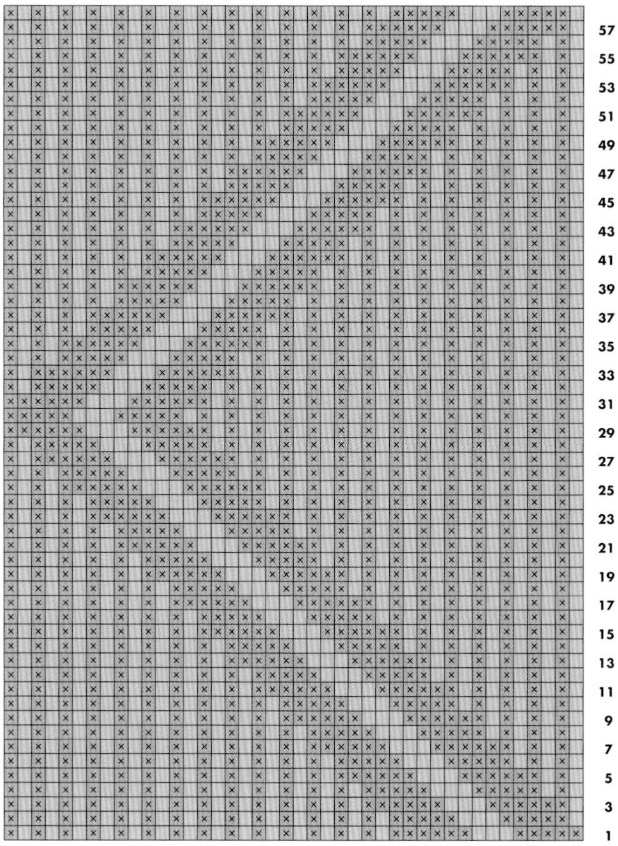

inc rnd once more—288 (312, 336, 360, 396) sts; 144 (156, 168, 180, 198) sts each for front and back; piece measures about 5½ (6¾, 8, 9¼, 10½)" (14 [17, 20.5, 23.5, 26.5] cm) from beg of vertical stripes and chart patt, not counting the solid-color hem section. Work even until piece measures 11 (11, 12½, 12½, 13¾)" (28 [28, 31.5, 31.5, 35] cm) from beg of vertical stripes and chart patt.

MARK ARMHOLES

With waste yarn, mark edge sts at each side of last rnd to indicate base of armholes. Cont for your size as foll:

For sizes 36" and 39": Work even until Rnds 1–58 of charts have been worked a total of 2 times, then work Rnds 1–30 once more—146 rnds completed above hem section; piece measures about 19½" (49.5 cm) above hem section.

For sizes 42" and 45": Work even until Rnds 1–66 of charts have been worked a total of 2 times, then work Rnds 1–34 once more—166 rnds completed above hem section; piece measures about 21¼" (51.5 cm) above hem section.

For size 49½": Work even until Rnds 1–74 of charts have been worked a total of 2 times, then work Rnds 1–38 once more—186 rnds completed above hem section; piece measures about 24¾" (63 cm) above hem section.

For all sizes: Place sts on separate holders for front and back.

SLEEVES

With B and smaller dpn, CO 62 (62, 70, 70, 78) sts. Pm and join for working in the rnd, being careful not to twist sts. Work even in St st for 1¼" (3.2 cm). Change to larger dpn. Set up edge sts and patt from chart as foll: *K1 with A, pm, work Sleeve chart (see pages 94 and 95) for your size over 59 (59, 67, 67, 75) sts, pm, k1 with A, k1 with B. Cont in patt, working vertical stripes of A and B at each side of chart as established, until Rnd 3 of chart has been completed. Beg on the next rnd, inc 1 st at each end of rnd, working inc'd sts into vertical stripes patt—2 sts inc'd. Work 2 rnds even. Cont in patt, rep the shaping of the last 3 rnds 35 (35, 41, 41, 47) more times, then work inc rnd once more, changing to larger 16" (40 cm) cir needle when there are too many sts to fit on dpn—136 (136, 156, 156, 176) sts. Work even until Rnds 1–58 (58,

66, 66, 74) of chart have been worked 2 times—116 (116, 132, 132, 148) rnds completed from beg of vertical stripes and chart; piece measures about 15½ (15½, 17¾, 17¾)" (39.5 [39.5, 45, 45, 50] cm) from beg of vertical stripes and chart.

ARMHOLE FACING

With A only, work in solid-color St st for ½" (1.3 cm) for armhole facing. Loosely BO all sts.

FINISHING
CUT FRONT NECK OPENING

Place center 56 (56, 56, 60, 64) sts at center back and front on holders, leaving rem 44 (50, 56, 60, 67) sts at each side on separate holders for shoulders. Measure down 1¾" (4.5 cm) from top of piece at center front. Baste the outline of a rounded front neck opening starting at one edge of the center, down to the center front, and back up to the other edge of the center sts. With sewing machine or by hand, sew two lines of small straight stitches along the front basting line. Cut out front neck opening about ¼" (6 mm) inside the basting line to leave a small seam allowance. Back neckline is not shaped; leave 56 (56, 56, 60, 64) back neck sts on holder.

CUT ARMHOLES

Baste a line of contrasting thread at each side of body between the edge sts of front and back from marked positions at base of each armhole to shoulder. With sewing machine or by hand, sew a line of small straight stitches one stitch away on each side of the basting line and across the bottom of the armhole. Sew over the same line of stitching again. Carefully cut open the armholes along the basting line from shoulder to base of armholes.

JOIN SHOULDERS

Place about 44 (50, 56, 60, 67) sts each for front and back left shoulders on ends of larger cir needle. *Note:* 1 or 2 sts at each cut edge may have been eliminated by the armhole steeks, so you may have fewer shoulder sts available. Turn work carefully inside out, and with right sides touching, use the three-needle bind-off technique (see Glossary, page 140) and single larger dpn to join left shoulders tog. Rep for right shoulder.

SET IN SLEEVES

Position the top of the sleeve against the cut armhole, matching center of sleeve to shoulder seam. With yarn threaded on a tapestry needle and RS facing, sew the last patt rnd at top of sleeve (just below the St st armhole facing) to cut edge of armhole 1 st inside the lines of stitching. On WS, smooth the armhole facing to cover the cut edge. With yarn threaded on a tapestry needle, sew facing in place.

NECKBAND
Place 56 (56, 56, 60, 64) sts held back neck sts on larger 16" (40 cm) cir, and with RS facing, join A and B to beg of sts. Work across 56 (56, 56, 60, 64) back neck sts in

 A

B

Chart 2 Size 49½"

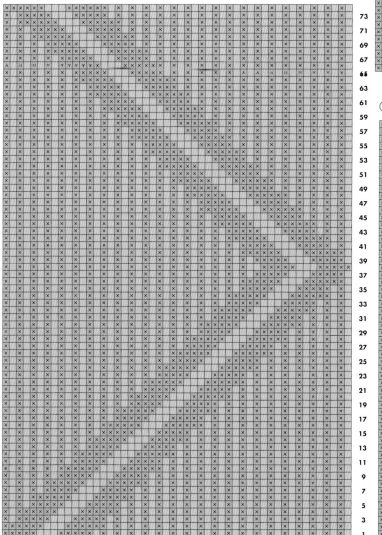

Chart 2 Sizes 42" and 45"

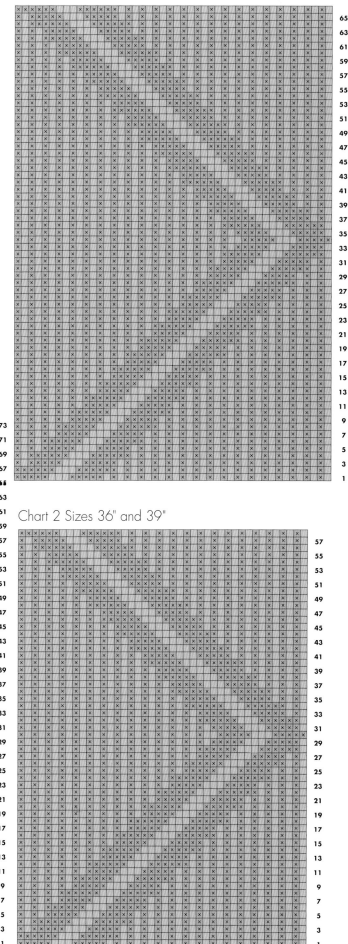

Chart 2 Sizes 36" and 39"

established vertical stripe patt, pick up and knit 56 (56, 56, 60, 64) sts along cut front neck opening in patt colors, picking up just below the stitching lines—112 (112, 112, 120, 128) sts. *Note:* If necessary, pick up an extra st at each shoulder seam in order to maintain the vertical stripes patt. Pm and join for working in the rnd. Work vertical stripe patt as established until neckband measures 2¾" (7 cm) from pick-up rnd or desired length.

Facing: Change to smaller 16" (40 cm) cir needle, and break off A. With B only, purl 1 rnd for turning ridge, then work even in St st until neckband measures 2¾" (7 cm) from turning ridge. BO all sts loosely.

Rolled edge: With smaller 16" (40 cm) cir needle, color B, and RS facing, pick up and knit 112 (112, 112, 120, 128) sts along purl "bumps" of turning ridge. Pm, and join for working in the rnd. Work even in St st for 6 rnds. BO all sts.

Fold lower body and sleeve hems to the inside along the lines where the fabric changes from solid to patterned. With yarn threaded on tapestry needle, sew hems in place. Fold neckband to inside along turning ridge and sew in place to cover cut edge of neck opening. Weave in loose ends. Carefully steam-press sweater under a damp cloth.

| × | A |
| ☐ | B |

Sleeve Size 49½"

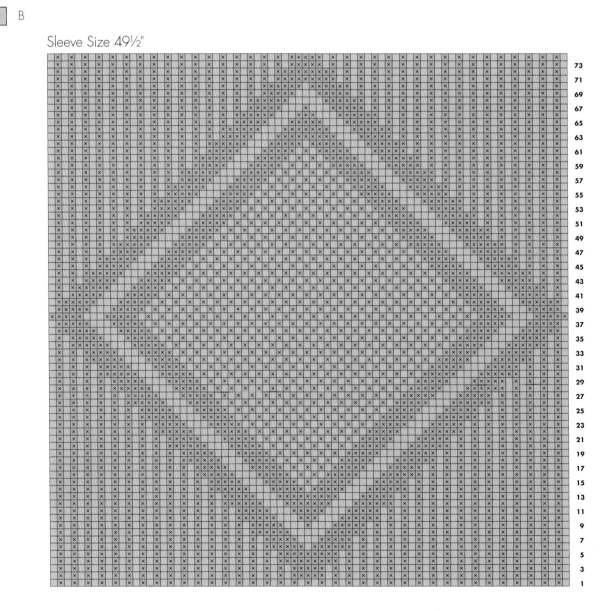

Sleeve Sizes 42" and 45"

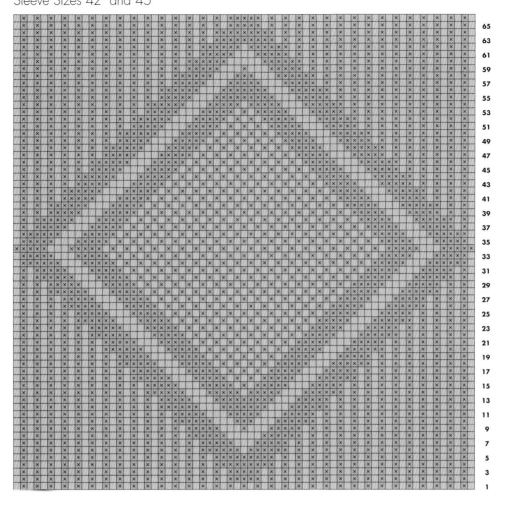

65
63
61
59
57
55
53
51
49
47
45
43
41
39
37
35
33
31
29
27
25
23
21
19
17
15
13
11
9
7
5
3
1

Sleeve Sizes 36" and 39"

57
55
53
51
49
47
45
43
41
39
37
35
33
31
29
27
25
23
21
19
17
15
13
11
9
7
5
3
1

STRANDED TWO-COLOR KNITTING

Stranded two-color knitting, also called jacquard or Fair Isle knitting, involves working with two colors at the same time, although in such a way that one color is stranded across the back (wrong side) of the work while the other color is being knitted. The keys to success are even tension (the unworked strands must have the same widthwise tension as the knitting) and consistent use of the two colors so that one color is the dominant color throughout.

This technique is used for Mali (page 72), Arrowheads (page 80), Zimbabwe (page 88), Nigeria (page 98), Zigzag (page 106), Shoowa (page 114), and Shoowa Vest (page 122).

DOMINANT COLOR

The manner in which you hold the two yarns in stranded knitting may result in the stitches of one color being slightly larger than the stitches of the other, causing them to "pop" out from the background on the right side of the work. The slightly more prominent stitches are said to be in the dominant color.

For best results, use the Continental method of knitting and hold both yarns in the left hand. Hold one color over the index finger and the other over both the index and middle fingers (Figure 1). It is worthwhile to learn this method as it offers several advantages:

- The two strands are not in contact with each other and therefore cannot tangle.
- The strand that is not worked (the "float") will have the same tension as the strand that is knitted, therefore the fabric is less likely to pucker.
- The strand that lies closest to the knitting (the one that lies over just the index finger), will be the primary strand in the pattern. The stitches made with this strand will be slightly larger than the others and therefore, this strand is designated the dominant color.

TO WORK STRANDED TWO-COLOR KNITTING

To practice, you will need needles and two colors of yarn—one light and one dark. Cast on 8 stitches with the light yarn. Place the yarns over the index and middle fingers of your left hand as shown in Figure 1 so that the light yarn is in the dominant position—furthest from your finger tip and draped over just your index finger. Alternate one stitch of each color in stockinette stitch as follows:

Right-side rows:

Step 1: Knit the first stitch with both colors held together.

Step 2: Insert the right needle through the second stitch and knit it with the light yarn (Figure 2).

Step 3: Insert the right needle through the next stitch, bring it over the light yarn, and knit the stitch with the dark yarn (Figure 3).

Alternate Steps 2 and 3 (working one stitch each of each color) in this manner to the last stitch. Knit the last stitch with both colors held together (Figure 4).

Wrong-side rows:

To keep the light yarn dominant on the right side of the piece while working wrong-side rows, rearrange the yarns in your left hand so that the dark yarn is positioned as the dominant color—so that the dark color is furthest from your fingertips and is draped over just the index finger.

Step 1: Knit the first stitch with both colors held together.

Step 2: Insert the needle under both yarns, then purl the next stitch with the dark yarn (Figure 5), pulling the stitch under the light yarn so that the light yarn remains on the wrong side of the work (Figure 6).

Step 3: Insert the needle under both yarns, purl the next stitch with the light yarn (Figure 7), catching the light yarn over the top of the dark yarn and pulling the stitch under the dark yarn so that the dark yarn remains on the wrong side of the work.

Alternate Steps 2 and 3 to the last stitch. Knit the last stitch with both colors held together (Figure 8).

To work stranded two-color knitting in rounds, the right side of the work will always face you and there will be no edge stitches. Therefore, you will always hold the two yarns the same way and will work every stitch with just one color.

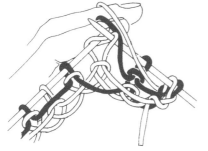

Figure 1

Figure 2

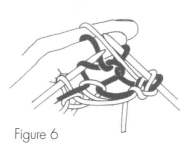

Figure 3

Figure 4

Figure 5

Figure 6

Figure 7

Figure 8

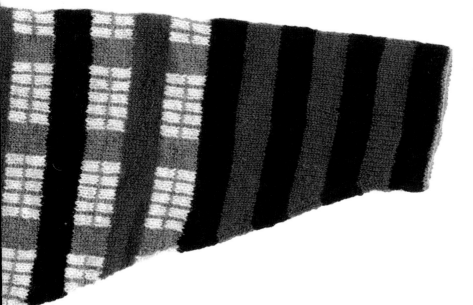

The pullover shown here mimics the African look of pieced strips of woven cloth by alternating bands of stranded two-color knitting with solid-color stripes. The sweater is worked in one piece from cuff to cuff, and except for the shaping of the tapered body sides, it is all worked in the round. Extra steek stitches are worked at the lower body and upper neck edges, then secured, cut open, and concealed with knitted facings. A zipper in the center front adds sporty versatility.

MATERIALS

SIZES 39 (43, 48)" (99 [109, 122] cm) finished chest/bust circumference. Shown in size 43" (109 cm).

YARN About 100 (125, 150) g each of four colors (A, B, C, and D), and 50 g of one color (E) of fingering-weight (CYCA Super Fine #1) yarn.

Shown here: Isager Tvinni (100% merino lambswool; 558 yd [510 m]/100 g): #30 black (A), #47 dark blue-gray (B), #6s beige heather (C), and #52s plum heather (D), 1 (2, 2) skein(s) each; #23s dark gray-khaki heather (E), 1 skein.

NEEDLES U.S. sizes 2 and 4 (3.0 and 3.5 mm): 16" and 24" or 32" (40 and 60 or 80 cm) circular (cir) and set of 4 or 5 double-pointed (dpn). Adjust needle size if necessary to obtain the correct gauge.

NOTIONS Stitch markers (m); tapestry needle; sharp-point sewing needle or sewing machine; contrasting basting thread for steeks; matching sewing thread for steeks and attaching zipper; 10" (25.5 cm) zipper for neck.

GAUGE 28½ sts and 36 rows = 4" (10 cm) in St st on larger needles.

NOTES

- Read about stranded two-color knitting on page 96. For this project, color C is the dominant color in the two-color stockinette pattern for the sleeves so the light rectangles will stand out on the darker background. Color D is the dominant color for the center of the body so the various darker motifs will stand out from the lighter background.

- To create a uniform fabric throughout, notice how you handle the yarns in order to make one color or the other the dominant color, and always use the yarns in the same manner when working in the round or knitting right-side rows. When purling wrong-side rows, reverse the positions of the two yarns in order to keep same color dominant. Experiment with your gauge swatch until you have achieved the desired effect.

RIGHT SLEEVE AND SIDE

With E and smaller dpn, CO 68 sts. Place marker (pm) and join for working in the rnd, being careful not to twist sts. Work in St st (knit every rnd) for sleeve facing until piece measures 1" (2.5 cm) from beg. Purl 1 rnd for turning ridge. Change to larger dpn. Join A and work in St st for 8 (11, 14) rnds.

SHAPE SLEEVE

Note: The sleeve stripes are worked at the same time as sleeve shaping; read the next section all the way through

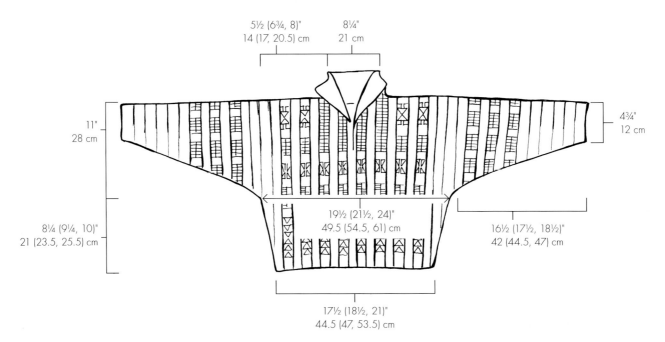

5½ (6¾, 8)"
14 (17, 20.5) cm

8¼"
21 cm

4¾"
12 cm

11"
28 cm

19½ (21½, 24)"
49.5 (54.5, 61) cm

16½ (17½, 18½)"
42 (44.5, 47) cm

8¼ (9¼, 10)"
21 (23.5, 25.5) cm

17½ (18½, 21)"
44.5 (47, 53.5) cm

before proceeding. Inc 1 st at each end of rnd as foll every 3 rnds 16 (22, 28) times: K1, M1 (see Glossary, page 140), knit to last st, M1, k1—2 sts inc'd. Change to larger 16" (40 cm) cir needle when there are too many sts to fit comfortably on dpn. *At the same time* work stripes as foll: *Work 8 (11, 14) rnds B, 8 (11, 14) rnds A; rep from * 2 more times—100 (112, 124) sts when all incs have been worked; 56 (77, 98) rnds and seven 8 (11, 14)-rnd stripes completed from turning ridge; piece measures about 6¼ (8½, 11)" (16 [21.5, 28] cm) from turning ridge. Join C and D and work Rnd 1 of Sleeve chart (see page 102), beg and ending where indicated for your size for right sleeve. *Note:* The next 55 patt rnds for sleeve are worked at the same time as the sleeve shaping continues; read the next section all the way through before proceeding. Cont sleeve shaping by inc 1 st at each end of rnd as before every 3 rnds 16 (16, 10) times, then every other rnd 3 (3, 7) times, working inc'd sts into patt. When this set of shaping instructions has been completed, work even without shaping to end of 55-rnd patt section. *At the same time,* work Rnds 2–11 of chart, knit 11 rnds with B, work Rnds 1–11 of chart, beg and ending where necessary to align the patt exactly over the previous patt, knit 11 rnds with A, work Rnds 1–11 of chart, aligning the patt again as necessary—138 (150, 158) sts; 55 rnds completed from beg of first Sleeve chart; 111 (132, 153) rnds completed

from turning ridge; piece measures about 12½ (14¾, 17)" (31.5 [37.5, 43] cm) from turning ridge. *Note:* The next series of stripes is worked at the same time as the sleeve is completed and the side is shaped; read the next section all the way through before proceeding. Work the stripe patt for next 43 rnds/rows for all sizes as foll: *10 rows B, 1 row E, 10 rows A,* 1 row E, rep from * to * once more—43 stripe rows. *At the same time* work shaping for your size over 43 rnds/rows as foll:

SIZE 39"

Inc 1 st at each side as before every other rnd 10 times—158 sts. Work 17 rnds even—148 rnds completed from turning ridge; sleeve measures about 16½" (42 cm) from turning ridge. Work St st back and forth in rows, changing to larger longer cir needle as necessary to accommodate new sts. Using the knitted method (see Glossary, page 139), CO 20 sts at beg of next 2 rows, then CO 19 sts at beg of next 4 rows—274 sts; 43 stripe rnds/rows completed; piece measures ¾" (2 cm) from end of sleeve. With RS facing, rejoin for working center body in the rnd; rnd begins at lower edge of front. *Note:* At beg of first rnd for center body, use the knitted method to CO 3 sts for steek, knit new steek sts, pm, then work as given for center body—277 sts after adding 3 steek sts.

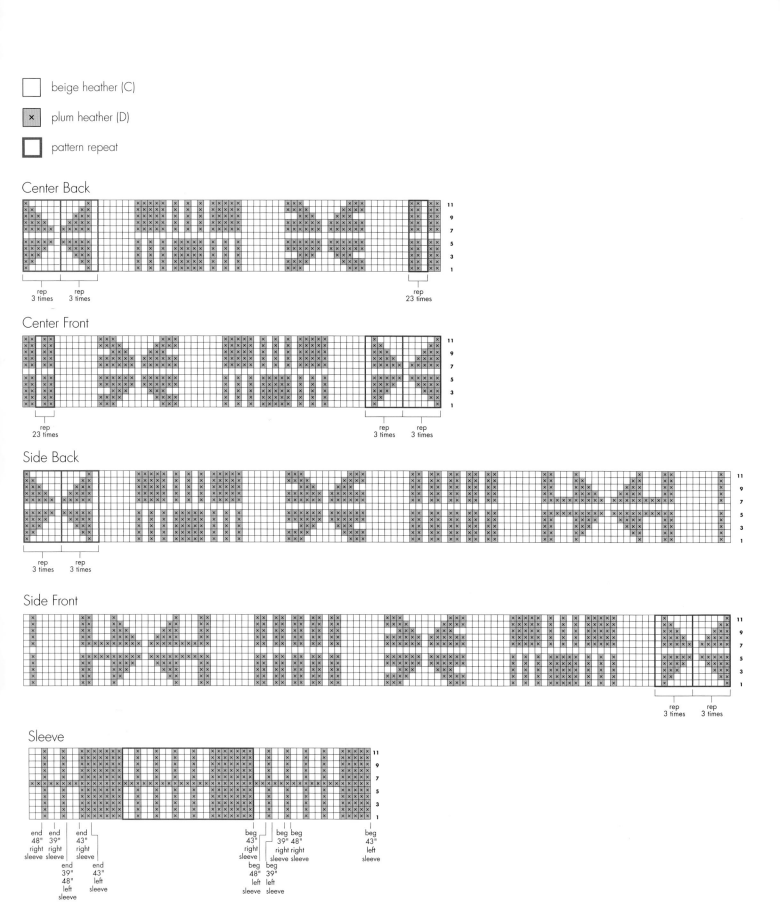

beige heather (C)

plum heather (D)

pattern repeat

Center Back

Center Front

Side Back

Side Front

Sleeve

SIZE 43"

Inc 1 st at each side as before every other rnd 4 times—158 sts. Work 17 rnds even—157 rnds completed from turning ridge; sleeve measures about 17½" (44.5 cm) from turning ridge. Work St st back and forth in rows, changing to larger longer cir needle as necessary to accommodate new sts. Using the knitted method (see Glossary, page 139), CO 10 sts at beg of next 4 rows, then CO 9 sts at beg of next 10 rows—288 sts. With RS facing, rejoin for working in the rnd; rnd begins at lower edge of front. *Next rnd:* Using the knitted method, CO 3 sts for steek, knit new steek sts, pm, work to end—291 sts: 288 body sts, 3 steek sts between markers. Work 3 more rnds even—43 stripe rnds/rows completed; piece measures 2" (5 cm) from end of sleeve.

SIZE 48"

Work 13 rnds even—166 rnds completed from turning ridge; sleeve measures about 18½" (47 cm) from turning ridge. Work St st back and forth in rows, changing to larger longer cir needle as necessary to accommodate new sts. Using the knitted method (see Glossary, page 139), CO 10 sts at beg of next 14 rows—298 sts. With RS facing, rejoin for working in the rnd; rnd begins at lower edge of front. *Next rnd:* Using the knitted method, CO 3 sts for steek, knit new steek sts, pm, work to end—301 sts: 298 body sts, 3 steek sts between markers. Work 15 more rnds even—43 stripe rnds/rows completed; piece measures 3¼" (8.5 cm) from end of sleeve.

CENTER BODY

For all sizes: Center body is worked over 277 (291, 301) sts, including steek sts. Join C and D. Work 3 steek sts, sl m, work 0 (7, 12) sts with C, work 137 sts according to Rnd 1 of Side Front chart, pm at shoulder line, work 137 sts according to Rnd 1 of Side Back chart, work 0 (7, 12) sts with C. Working steek sts and sts outside patt with C, work Rnds 2–11 of charts. Change to B and knit 10 rnds. Change to C and D and work Rnds 1–11 of Side Front and Back charts again. Change to A and knit 10 rnds—piece measures about 5½ (6¾, 8)" (14 [17, 20.5] cm) from end of sleeve.

SHAPE NECK

Work 3 steek sts, work 0 (7, 12) sts with C, work first 137 sts of Rnd 1 of Center Front chart, use the knitted method and D to CO 43 sts onto left-hand needle, work rem 20 sts of Center Front chart over new sts, pm, work 3 neck steek sts with D, pm, work 157 sts of Center Back chart, work 0 (7, 12) sts with C—320 (334, 344) sts: 3 steek sts at top of neck and lower edge, 157 (164, 169) sts each for front and back. Working steek sts and sts outside patt in established colors, work Rnds 2–11 of charts. Change to B and knit 10 rnds. Change to C and D and work Rnds 1–11 of Center Front and Back charts once more. Change to A and knit 4 rnds.

FRONT NECK SLIT

With A, k3 lower edge steek sts, k86 (93, 98) front sts, BO 71 sts, knit to end. *Next rnd:* With A, knit to gap formed by binding off in previous rnd. Use the knitted method to CO 71 sts onto left-hand needle, k71 new sts, knit to end. With A, knit 4 rnds. Change to C and D and work Rnds 1–11 of Center Front and Back charts once more. Change to B and knit 10 rnds. Change to C and D and work first 10 rnds of Center Front and Back charts once more. *Next rnd:* (Rnd 11 of charts), work in patt to 20 sts before first marker for neck steeks, BO 43 neck sts with D, replace single shoulder marker, work in patt to end—277 (291, 301) sts; 274 (288, 298) body sts, 3 steek sts at lower edge. Change to A and knit 10 rnds. Change to C and D and work Rnds 1–11 of Side Front and Back charts. Change to B and knit 10 rnds. Change to C and D and work Rnds 1–11 of Side Front and Back charts once more—piece measures about 4¾" (12 cm) from sts BO at end of neck.

LEFT SLEEVE AND SIDE

Note: The next series of stripes is worked at the same time as the side shaping and left sleeve; read the next section all the way through before proceeding. Work the stripe patt for next 43 rnds/rows for all sizes as foll: *10 rows A, 1 row E, 10 rows B,* 1 row E, rep from * to * once more—43 stripe rows. *At the same time,* work shaping for your size over 43 rnds/rows as foll:

SIZE 39"

Working back and forth in rows, BO 22 sts at beg of next row (3 steek sts plus 19 body sts), then BO 19 sts at beg next 3 rows, then BO 20 sts at beg next 2 rows—158 sts rem; piece measures about ¾" (2 cm) from beg of side shaping. With RS facing, rejoin for working in the rnd, and pm for beg of rnd. Work 17 rnds even.

Shape sleeve: Dec 1 st at each end of rnd as foll every other rnd 10 times: K1, k2tog, knit to last 3 sts, ssk, k1—

138 sts rem; 43 stripe rnds completed. Change to larger 16" (40 cm) cir needle and dpn when there are too few sts to fit comfortably on longer cir needle.

SIZE 43"

Work 4 rnds even. Working back and forth in rows, BO 12 sts at beg of next row (3 steek sts plus 9 body sts), then BO 9 sts at beg of next 9 rows, then BO 10 sts at beg of next 4 rows—158 sts; piece measures about 2" (5 cm) from beg of side shaping. With RS facing, rejoin for working in the rnd, and pm for beg of rnd. Work 17 rnds even.

Shape sleeve: Dec 1 st at each end of rnd as foll every other rnd 4 times: K1, k2tog, knit to last 3 sts, ssk, k1—150 sts rem; 43 stripe rnds completed. Change to larger 16" (40 cm) cir needle and dpn when there are too few sts to fit comfortably on longer cir needle.

SIZE 48"

Work 16 rnds even. Working back and forth in rows, BO 13 sts at beg of next row (3 steek sts plus 10 body sts), then BO 10 sts at beg of next 13 rows—158 sts rem; piece measures about 3¼" (8.5 cm) from beg of side shaping. With RS facing, rejoin for working in the rnd, and pm for beg of rnd. Work 13 rnds even—43 stripe rnds completed.

ALL SIZES

Note: The next 55 patt rnds for sleeve are worked at the same time as the sleeve shaping continues; read the next section all the way through before proceeding. Work 1 (1, 11) rnd(s) even—still 138 (150, 158) sts. Cont sleeve shaping by dec 1 st at each end of rnd every other rnd 3 (3, 7) times, then every 3 rnds 16 (16, 10) times. *At the same time,* beg and ending where indicated for your size for left sleeve, work Rnd 1 of Sleeve chart. Cont decs, work Rnds 2–11 of Sleeve chart. Knit 11 rnds with A, work Rnds 1–11 of chart, beg and ending where necessary to align the patt exactly over the previous patt, knit 11 rnds with B, work Rnds 1–11 of chart, aligning the patt again as necessary—100 (112, 124) sts rem; 55 rnds completed from beg of first Sleeve chart; 92 (80, 68) rnds completed

from where work was rejoined for working sleeve in the rnd; sleeve measures about 10¼ (9, 7½)" (26 [23, 19] cm). *Note:* The final sleeve stripes are worked at the same time as sleeve shaping continues; read the next section all the way through before proceeding. Dec 1 st at each end of rnd every 3 rnds 16 (22, 28) times. *At the same time,* work stripes as foll: *8 (11, 14) rnds A, 8 (11, 14) rnds B; rep from * 2 more times—68 sts for all sizes. Change to A and work 8 (11, 14) rnds even—148 (157, 166) sleeve rnds completed, sleeve measures about 16½ (17½, 18½)" (42 [44.5, 47] cm). Change to E and smaller dpn. Knit 1 rnd, then purl 1 rnd for turning ridge. Work even in St st for sleeve facing until piece measures 1" (2.5 cm) from turning ridge. BO alls sts.

FINISHING
Carefully steam-press the sweater under a damp cloth.

CUT STEEKS
Baste a line of contrasting thread along the center of the 3-st steeks at lower edge of sweater and top of neck opening. With sewing machine or by hand, sew a line of small straight stitches one stitch away on each side of the basting line. Sew over the same two lines of stitching again. Carefully cut open the lower edge and top of neck opening along the basting lines.

COLLAR FACING
With smaller 16" (40 cm) cir needle, E, and RS facing, pick up and knit about 118 sts around top of neck opening, picking up just beyond the stitching lines. Working back and forth in rows, knit 1 WS row for turning ridge, then work even in St st until facing measures 3" (7.5 cm) from pick-up row, ending with a WS row. On the next row, k30, BO center 58 sts for back neck, k30—30 sts at each side. Working each side separately, CO 5 sts on each side of back neck gap—35 sts at each side. Cont in St st, dec 1 st at each back neck edge (not outer selvedges) every 6 rows 11 times—24 sts. Work even until facing measures 10¾" (27.5 cm) from turning ridge. BO all sts.

SIDE AND NECK SEAMS
With yarn threaded on a tapestry needle and using the mattress st (see Glossary, page 141), sew side seams and short seams on either side of neck.

LOWER EDGING
With smaller long cir needle, E, and RS facing, pick up and knit 250 (264, 300) sts along lower edge of sweater, picking up just beyond the stitching lines. Pm and join for working in the rnd. Purl 1 rnd for turning ridge. Work in St st until lower edging measures 1½" (3.8 cm) from pick-up rnd. BO all sts.

ZIPPER
Align top of 10" (20.5 cm) zipper with turning ridge of collar facing. With sewing needle and thread, sew zipper in place (see Glossary, page 141). With yarn threaded on a tapestry needle, close any gap at center front below zipper, if necessary. With sewing needle and thread, sew center front edges of collar facing to zipper tape so as to cover zipper tape with facing. With yarn threaded on a tapestry needle, tack shaped edges of facing to inside of sweater as invisibly as possible.

Fold lower edging and sleeve facings to WS along turning ridges. With yarn threaded on a tapestry needle, sew in place. Weave in loose ends. Steam-press all edges and seams.

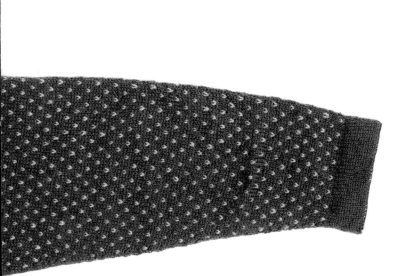

This tunic-style pullover is modeled after a two-color woven basket from the Lake Kariba region in Zimbabwe. The lower edges of the front and back are worked separately, then the two pieces are joined and the color work pattern is worked in the round to the base of the front neck opening, with extra steek stitches added at the sides for the armholes. Stitches are placed on hold at center front, and work continues back and forth while the front neck is shaped. The stitches along the armholes are secured, then the steeks are cut open. The sleeves are worked in the round in a different pattern and sewn into the cut armholes. Worked last, the collar and contrasting collar facing are finished with a zipper. The short slits at the lower body sides are also finished with zippers.

MATERIALS

SIZES 35½ (38½, 42, 46, 50½)" (90 [98, 106.5, 117, 128.5] cm) finished chest/bust circumference. Shown in size 38½" (98 cm).

YARN About 225 (250, 275, 300, 325) g each of two colors of fingering-weight (CYCA Super Fine #1) yarn.

Shown here: Isager Tvinni (100% merino lambswool; 558 yd [510 m]/100 g): #47 dark blue-gray (A), 3 (3, 3, 4, 4) skeins.

Isager Highland (100% pure new wool; 612 yd [560 m]/100 g): #8 blue topaz (medium blue heather; B), 3 (3, 3, 3, 4) skeins.

Also shown in Tvinni #30 black (A) and #32s burgundy heather (B) behind basket on page 107.

NEEDLES U.S. sizes 1 and 2 (2.25 and 3 mm): straight, 32" (80 cm) circular (cir), and set of 4 or 5 double-pointed (dpn). Adjust needle size if necessary to obtain the correct gauge.

NOTIONS Stitch markers (m); tapestry needle; removable marker or safety pins; sharp-point sewing needle or sewing machine; contrasting basting thread for steeks; matching sewing thread for steeks and attaching zipper; 8" (20.5 cm) zipper for neck; two 2" (5 cm) zippers for side slits (optional).

GAUGE 32 sts and 32 rows/rnds = 4" (10 cm) in stranded two-color St st from Front and Back charts using larger needles; 28 sts and 30 rnds = 4" (10 cm) in stranded two-color St st from Dots chart using larger needles.

NOTES

- Read about stranded two-color knitting on page 96. For this project, color B is the dominant color. To create a uniform fabric throughout, notice how you handle the yarns in order to make B the dominant color, and always use the yarns in the same manner when working in the round or knitting right-side rows. When purling wrong-side rows, reverse the positions of the two yarns in order to keep color B dominant. Experiment with your gauge swatch until you have achieved the desired effect.

LOWER EDGING (MAKE 2)

With A and smaller cir needle, CO 134 (146, 154, 170, 186) sts. Working patt from Dots chart (see page 110) back and forth in rows, rep Rows 1–6 three times, then work Rows 1 and 2 once more—20 rows completed; piece measures about 2¼" (5.5 cm) from beg. With A, purl across the next RS row for turning ridge. Work in St st with A only until piece measures 2¼" (5.5 cm) from turning ridge, ending with a WS row. Place sts on holder. Make a second piece the same as the first, leaving sts on needle.

BODY
JOINING ROUND

Change to larger cir needle. Work across sts on needle as foll for back: K1 with A (edge st; work in A throughout), [k1 with B, k1 with A] 25 (28, 30, 34, 38) times, place marker (pm), work center 32 sts according to Rnd 1 of Back chart (see page 110), pm, [k1 with B, k1 with A] 25 (28, 30, 34, 38) times, k1 with A (edge st; work in A throughout), pm for left side "seam." Return 134 (146, 154, 170, 186) held sts of other edging piece to smaller cir needle, and with larger cir needle cont across these sts for front as foll: K1 with A (edge st, work in A throughout), rep [k1 with B, k1 with A] to last st, k1 with A (edge st,

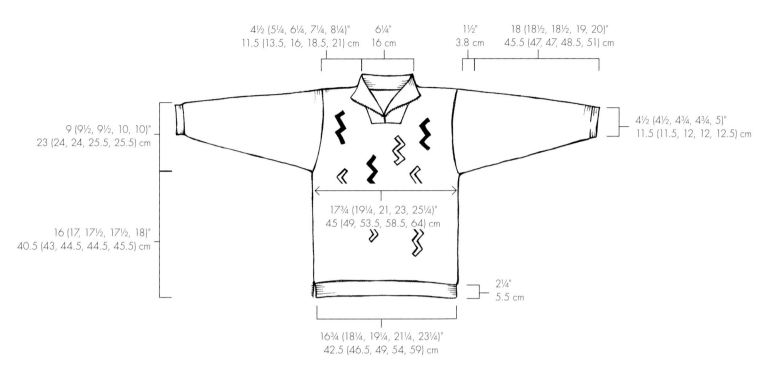

4½ (5¼, 6¼, 7¼, 8¼)"
11.5 (13.5, 16, 18.5, 21) cm

6¼"
16 cm

1½"
3.8 cm

18 (18½, 18½, 19, 20)"
45.5 (47, 47, 48.5, 51) cm

9 (9½, 9½, 10, 10)"
23 (24, 24, 25.5, 25.5) cm

4½ (4½, 4¾, 4¾, 5)"
11.5 (11.5, 12, 12, 12.5) cm

17¾ (19¼, 21, 23, 25¼)"
45 (49, 53.5, 58.5, 64) cm

16 (17, 17½, 17½, 18)"
40.5 (43, 44.5, 44.5, 45.5) cm

2¼"
5.5 cm

16¾ (18¼, 19¼, 21¼, 23¼)"
42.5 (46.5, 49, 54, 59) cm

work in A throughout), pm, and join for working in the rnd—268 (292, 308, 340, 372) sts; "seam" markers are in the center of the edge sts at each side; rnd begins at right side seam at beg of back sts.

Rnd 1: K1 with A (edge st), rep [k1 with A, k1 with B] to marker, work center 32 sts according to next rnd of Back chart, rep [k1 with A, k1 with B] to 1 st before marker, k1 with A (edge st), slip (sl) left side marker, k1 with A (edge st), rep [k1 with A, k1 with B] to last st, k1 with A (edge st).

Rnd 2: K1 with A (edge st), rep [k1 with B, k1 with A] to marker, work center 32 sts according to next rnd of Back chart, rep [k1 with B, k1 with A] to 1 st before marker, k1 with A (edge st), slip (sl) left side marker, k1 with A (edge st), rep [k1 with B, k1 with A] to last st, k1 with A (edge st).

Inc rnd: Beg on the next rnd, inc 1 st at each side of both front and back, working incs inside edge sts, working inc'd sts into alternating "checkerboard" patt, and maintaining edge sts in A throughout—4 sts inc'd. Cont in established patts and work 3 rnds even. Cont in patt, rep the shaping of the last 4 rnds 2 (2, 5, 5, 6) more times, then work inc rnd once more—284 (308, 336, 368, 404) sts; 142 (154, 168, 184, 202) sts each for front and back; piece measures about 4 (4, 5½, 5½, 6)" (10 [10, 14, 14, 15] cm) from turning ridge. *Note:* When Rnd 18 of Back chart has

been completed, cont to rep Rnds 1–18 of chart to end. Mark center 116 sts of front for placement of Front chart. If necessary, work 1 more rnd so that first st of marked 116 sts has just been worked with B, so that when Front chart is introduced it will flow uninterrupted into the established checkerboard patt. Introduce Front chart (see page 111) on next rnd as foll: Work edge sts, checkerboard, and back patt to marked front sts, work Rnd 1 of Front chart over next 116 sts, work in checkerboard patt and edge st as established to end. Work even in patt until piece measures 16 (17, 17½, 17½, 18)" (40.5 [43, 44.5, 44.5, 45.5] cm) from turning ridge. On the next rnd, work in patt to last st of back, *k1 with A (edge st), M1 with A (see Glossary, page 140)*, work in patt to last st of front, rep from * to * once more —2 sts inc'd; 286 (310, 338, 370, 406) sts; 143 (155, 169, 185, 203) sts each for front and back; 3 sts in color A at each side. Mark inc'd st at each side with waste yarn to indicate center st for armhole steek at base of armhole; work inc'd sts with A to end.

SHAPE ARMHOLES

Cont in patt in the rnd, beg on the next rnd dec 1 st at each side of front and back inside edge sts every rnd 6 times, then every 4 rnds 4 more times—4 sts dec'd each dec rnd; 40 sts dec'd total; 246 (270, 298, 330, 366) sts rem; 123 (135, 149, 165, 183) sts each for front and back. Work even in patt until piece measures 4½ (5, 5, 5½, 5½)"

Back

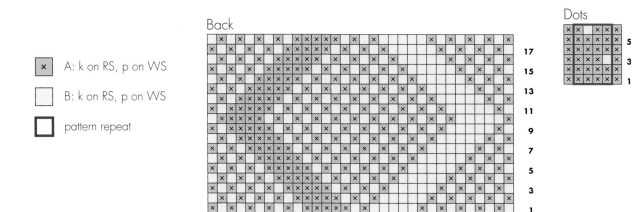

Dots

(11.5 [12.5, 12.5, 14, 14] cm) from armhole markers. Mark center 28 front checkerboard sts for front neck opening.

SHAPE FRONT NECK

Work edge sts, checkerboard, and front and back patt to marked front sts, place center 28 sts on holder, work front patt, checkerboard, and edge st to end—218 (242, 270, 302, 338) sts: 3 edge sts for front (1 at beg and 2 at end of front), 46 (52, 59, 67, 76) patt sts on either side of front opening, 123 (135, 149, 165, 183) sts for back. Working back and forth in rows, cont patts as established, and *at the same time* dec 1 st at each neck edge every 3 rows 11 times—196 (220, 248, 280, 316) sts; 3 edge sts for front;

35 (41, 48, 56, 65) patt sts on either side of front opening. *Note:* When Row 154 of Front chart has been completed, cont across all front sts in checkerboard patt; Back chart will cont as established to end. Work even until armholes measure 9 (9½, 9½, 10, 10)" (23 [24, 24, 25.5, 25.5] cm). Place sts on holder.

CUT ARMHOLE STEEKS

Baste a line of contrasting thread along the center of the 3 edge sts at each side. With sewing machine or by hand, sew a line of small straight stitches one stitch away on each side of the basting line and across the bottom of the armhole. Sew over the same line of stitching again.

151
141
131
121
111
101
91
81
71
61
51
41
31
21
11
1

Carefully cut open the armholes along the basting line from shoulder to base of armholes.

JOIN SHOULDERS

Divide rem 122 (134, 148, 164, 182) sts for back onto 3 holders: 50 sts for back neck and rem sts evenly divided on holders at sides. Place about 36 (42, 49, 57, 66) sts each for front and back left shoulders on ends of larger cir needle. *Note:* 1 or 2 sts at each cut edge may have been eliminated by the armhole steeks, so fewer shoulder sts may be available. Turn work carefully inside out, and with right sides touching, use the three-needle bind-off technique (see Glossary, page 140) and spare dpn to join left shoulders tog. Rep for right shoulder. Leave 50 sts for back neck on holder.

COLLAR
LEFT FRONT COLLAR

Transfer 14 sts from left half of held front neck sts to larger straight needles, and join B with RS facing. Work back and forth in St st, keeping 1 edge st at each side in garter st (knit every row), and *at the same time* inc 1 st at side of neck (beg of RS rows, end of WS rows) every 3 rows 11 times—25 sts. Work even until collar measures 4½" (11.5 cm) measured along the straight selvedge at center front, or same length as front from beg of neck shaping to shoulders. Make a note of how many rows you work even after the shaping has been completed so that you can work the collar facing to match. Place sts on holder.

RIGHT FRONT COLLAR

Transfer 14 sts from right half of held front neck sts to larger straight needles, and join B with RS facing. Work back and forth in St st, keeping 1 edge st at each side in garter st, and *at the same time* inc 1 st at side of neck (end of RS rows, beg of WS rows) every 3 rows 11 times—25 sts. Work even until right front collar measures same as left front collar, ending with a WS row.

JOIN LEFT AND RIGHT COLLARS

(RS) With B, knit across 25 right front collar sts, place 50 held back neck sts on larger needle with RS facing, knit across 50 back neck sts, place 25 held left front collar sts on larger needle with RS facing, and knit across 25 left

Dots chart in the rnd, work Rnds 1–6 once, then work Rnds 1–5 once more—11 rnds completed; piece measures about 1¼" (3.2 cm) from beg. With A, purl next rnd for turning ridge. Work in St st with A only until piece measures 1¼" (3.2 cm) from turning ridge. Change to larger dpn. Beg with Rnd 1, work in dots patt from chart for 3 rnds. *Inc rnd:* Work 1 st with A, M1, work in patt to last st, M1, work 1 st with A—2 sts inc'd. Cont in patt, inc 1 st at each end of rnd in this manner every 4 rnds 17 (12, 17, 10, 23) more times, then every 3 rnds 14 (22, 15, 26, 11) times, working inc'd sts into dots patt, and maintaining 1 st at each end of rnd in A throughout—126 (132, 132, 140, 140) sts. Work even until sleeve measures 18 (18½, 18½, 19, 20)" (45.5 [47, 47, 48.5, 51] cm) from turning ridge.

SHAPE CAP

At beg of next rnd, BO 4 sts, work in patt to end—122 (128, 128, 136, 136) sts. Working back and forth in rows, BO 4 sts at beg of next 11 rows—78 (84, 84, 92, 92) sts rem. BO all sts.

FINISHING

Fold lower edge and sleeve hems to WS along turning rows. With yarn threaded on a tapestry needle, sew invisibly in place. If not using zippers at sides, sew the open selvedges of each lower edging with yarn threaded on a tapestry needle, leaving short slits at each side.

ZIPPER

For zippered side slits, align top of each short zipper with turning ridge of lower edging, insert zipper tape between layers of lower edging, and with sewing needle and thread, sew in place (see Glossary, page 141). With yarn threaded on a tapestry needle, sew sleeves into steeked armholes. Align top of 8" (20.5 cm) zipper with dividing line between collar and collar facing. With sewing needle and thread, sew in place. With yarn threaded on a tapestry needle, close any gap at center front below zipper, if necessary. With sewing needle and thread, sew center front edges of collar facing to zipper tape so as to cover zipper tape with facing.

With yarn threaded on a tapestry needle, tack shaped lower edge of facing to inside of sweater as invisibly as possible. Weave in loose ends. Steam-press all edges and seams.

front collar sts—100 sts. Work even in St st until collar measures 2¾" (7 cm) measured straight up from center of back neck, ending with a WS row, and dec 2 sts evenly in last row—98 sts.

FACING

Join A and work in patt from Dots chart until piece measures 2¾" (7 cm) from beg of dots patt, ending with a WS row. *Next row:* (RS) Cont in dots patt, work 24 sts in patt for right front facing, join second ball of each color, BO center 50 sts, work 24 sts in patt for left front facing—24 sts at each side. Working each side separately in dots patt, work even for the same number of rows as for collar. Dec 1 st at side edge on either side of back neck gap every 3 rows 11 times—13 sts rem at each side; piece measures about 9" (23 cm) from beg of collar fronts, and 4½" (11.5 cm) from beg of dots patt measured along straight selvedge at each side. BO all sts.

SLEEVES

With A and smaller dpn, CO 62 (62, 66, 66, 70) sts. Pm and join for working in the rnd. Working patt from

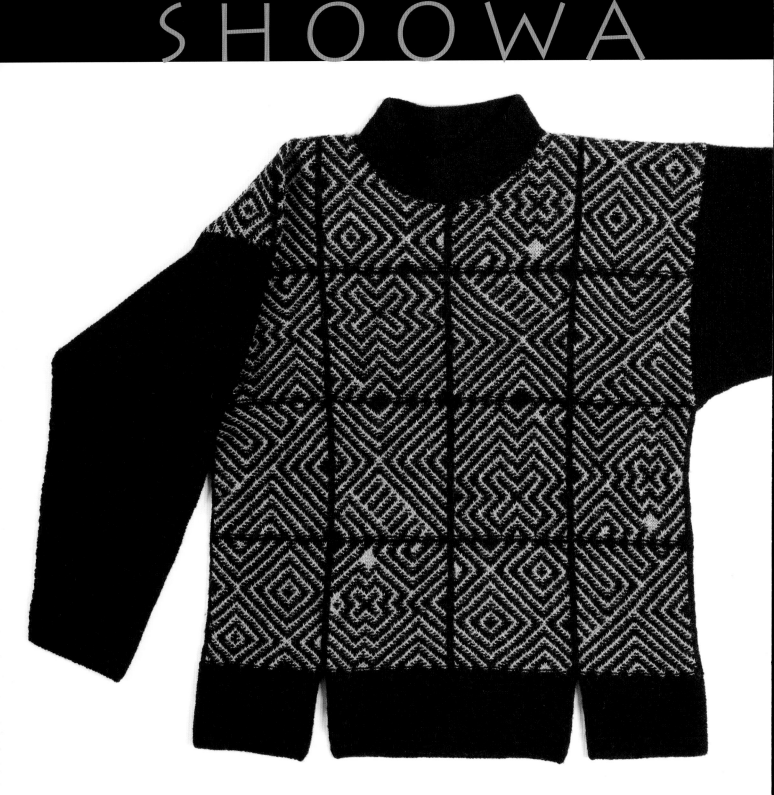

The Shoowa tribe from the Congo produces textiles made up of abstract geometric patterns embroidered on top of woven cloth. Close juxtaposition of the motifs gives a mosaic look to the overall cloth. On this long pullover, a similar look is achieved by arranging two-color pattern blocks in windowpane fashion on the front and back. Each two-color block is worked in a combination of knit and purl stitches for a feather-stitch effect. The technique is simpler than it looks— the main-color stitches are worked in stockinette, the contrasting-color stitches in reverse stockinette stitch. The lower body edge of the sweater is worked in four separate pieces that are joined together at the base of the pattern work, with slits at the lower front and back. The edging stitches are joined and the body is worked in the round to the shoulders, with steeks added for the armhole and neck openings. The garter-stitch sleeves are knitted in rows and sewn into the armholes; the front neck is cut to shape and finished with a simple garter-stitch band.

Hansjörg Mayer

MATERIALS

SIZES 46 (52)" (117 [132] cm) finished chest/bust circumference. Shown in size 46" (117 cm).

YARN About 575 (650) g main color (MC), and 150 (150) g contrasting color (CC) of fingering-weight (CYCA Super Fine #1) yarn.

Shown here: Isager Tvinni Alpaca (50% lambswool, 50% alpaca; 558 yd [510 m]/100 g): #30 black, 3 (4) skeins.
Isager Spinni (100% pure new wool; 667 yd [610 m]/100 g): #30 black, 3 (3) skeins.
Isager Tvinni (100% merino lambswool; 558 yd [510 m]/100 g): #7s medium brown heather, 2 (2) skeins.
Note: Use 1 strand each of Tvinni Alpaca and Spinni held together for MC; use a single strand of Tvinni for CC.

NEEDLES Lower edging—U.S. size 2 (3 mm): straight. Body, sleeves, and neckband—U.S. size 4 (3.5 mm): straight, and 16" (40 cm) and 32" (80 cm) circular (cir). Adjust needle size if necessary to obtain the correct gauge.

NOTIONS Stitch markers (m); stitch holders; tapestry needle; removable markers or safety pins; sharp-point sewing needle or sewing machine; contrasting basting thread for steeks; matching sewing thread for steeks.

GAUGE 28 sts and 54 rows = 4" (10 cm) in garter st with MC using larger needles; 29 sts and 33½ rows = 4" (10 cm) in charted two-color pattern stitch worked in the rnd using larger needles; each pattern block (40 sts and 46 rnds) measures about 5½" (14 cm) square.

Pattern Placement

8	4	5	2
3	10	9	8
1	7	6	5
4	3	2	1

NOTES

• MC always refers to a double strand of Tvinni Alpaca and Spinni held together; CC always refers to a single strand of Tvinni.

• Read about stranded two-color knitting on page 96. When working the chart patterns, carry the unused color loosely on the wrong side of the work; strands should never float across the right side of the fabric.

LOWER EDGING

With MC and smaller straight needles, CO 82 sts.

Row 1: (WS) P1, sl 1 as if to purl (pwise) with yarn in front (wyf), knit to last 2 sts, sl 1 pwise wyf, k1.

Row 2: (RS) P1, knit to end.

Rep Rows 1 and 2 until piece measures 4" (10 cm) from CO, ending with a WS row. Place sts on holder. *For size 46":* Make 3 more 82-st pieces the same way. *For size 52":* Make 1 more 82-st piece, then make 2 wider pieces by casting on 102 sts. *For both sizes:* Slip all 4 pieces to longer cir with RS facing without working them, arranging the 82-st and 102-st pieces for size 52" so that the first and third sections to be worked are 102-st pieces,

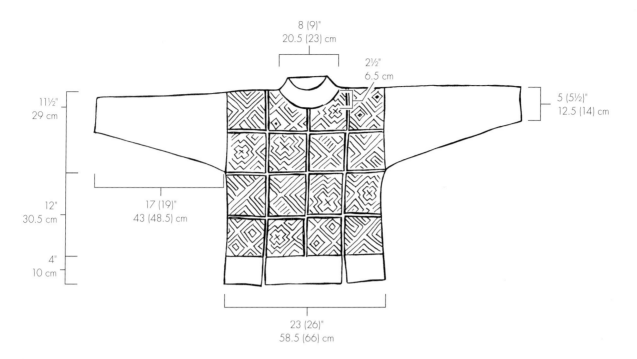

and the second and fourth sections to be worked are 82-st pieces—328 (368) sts. Work in the rnd for your size as foll:

Size 46": *K40, place marker (pm), k2, pm, k40, pm, use the backward loop method (see Glossary, page 139), to CO 2 sts, pm; rep from * 3 more times—336 sts: eight 40-st sections and eight 2-st sections.

Size 52": *K40, place marker (pm), k2, pm, k18, pm, k2, pm, k40, use the backward loop method (see Glossary, page 139) to CO 2 sts, pm, k40, pm, k2, pm, k40, pm, CO 2 sts; rep from * once more—376 sts: eight 40-st sections, ten 2-st sections, and two 18-st sections.

Both sizes: Next rnd: *P40, k2, p0 (18), k0 (2), [p40, k2] 3 times; rep from * once more—still 336 (376) sts. Break yarn. Sl the first 42 (51) sts of rnd to right-hand needle without working them; rnd now begins at left side "seam" at beg of a 40-st section for size 46"; in the middle of an 18-st section for size 52".

BODY

Note: To the end of the body, work all 2-st marked sections in St st (knit every rnd) with MC, and work the 18-st marked section at each side for size 52" in garter st (knit 1 rnd, purl 1 rnd) with MC. Join MC and CC. Establish patt and work Rnd 1 of charts (see pages 119–121) as foll: Work 0 (9) garter sts, 0 (2) St sts, *40 sts of Chart 1, 2 St sts, 40 sts Chart 2, 2 St sts, 40 sts Chart 3, 2 St sts, 40 sts

Chart 4, 2 St sts,* 0 (18) garter sts, 0 (2) St sts; rep from * to * once more to last 0 (9) sts, end 0 (9) garter sts. Cont in established patts until Rnd 46 of charts has been completed. *Framing rnd:* With MC only, work 0 (9) garter sts, k168 (170), work 0 (18) garter sts, k168 (170), work 0 (9) garter sts. Rep the framing rnd 2 more times—3 rnds total completed from end of charts. Establish the next tier of patt blocks as before, this time working Charts 5, 6, 7, and 1 in that order (see diagram for pattern placement, page 116). When Rnd 46 of the second tier of blocks has been completed, work 2 framing rnds as before with MC. Work 1 more framing rnd with MC as foll for your size to set up steek sts:

Size 46": K167, using the backward loop method, CO 3 steek sts, k168, CO 3 steek sts, k1—342 sts; 3 steek sts in center of 2-st section at each side.

Size 52": Using the backward loop method, CO 3 steek sts, work 9 garter sts, k170, work 9 garter sts, CO 3 steek sts, work 9 garter sts, k170 sts, work 9 garter sts—382 sts; 3 steek sts in center of 18-st garter section at each side.

Both sizes: Work steek sts in St st with MC to end of body. Establish the third tier of patt blocks as before, this time working Charts 8, 9, 10, and 3 in that order. When Rnd 46 of the third tier of blocks has been completed, work 3 framing rnds with MC. Establish the fourth tier of patt blocks as before, this time working Charts 2, 5, 4, and 8 in that order. When Rnd 46 of the fourth tier of blocks has

from top of piece at center front. Baste the outline of a rounded front neck opening starting at one edge of the center 58 (64) sts, down to the center front, and back up to the other edge of the center 58 (64) sts. With sewing machine or by hand, sew two lines of small straight sts along the front basting line. Cut out front neck opening about ¼" (6 mm) inside the basting line to leave a small seam allowance. Back neckline is not shaped.

CUT ARMHOLES

Baste a line of contrasting thread along the center of the 3-st steek at each side. With sewing machine or by hand, sew a line of small straight sts one st away on each side of the basting line. Sew over the same two lines of stitching again. Carefully cut open the armholes along the basting line from base of steek sts (where they were CO) to top of shoulder.

JOIN SHOULDERS

Place about 56 (63) held front shoulder sts on larger straight needle and about 56 (63) corresponding back shoulder sts on larger straight needle. *Note:* 1 or 2 sts at each cut edge may have been eliminated by the armhole steeks so fewer shoulder sts may be available. Turn work carefully inside out and with right sides touching, use the three-needle method (see Glossary, page 140) and spare cir needle to join shoulders tog. Rep for other shoulder.

SET IN SLEEVES

Position the top of the sleeve against the cut armhole with the sleeve oriented so that the knit side of the St st armhole facing shows on the WS of the garment, and matching the center of the sleeve top to shoulder seam. With yarn threaded on a tapestry needle and RS facing, sew the last row of garter st at top of sleeve (just below the St st armhole facing) to cut edge of armhole 1 st inside the lines of stitching. On WS, smooth the armhole facing to cover the cut edge. With yarn threaded on a tapestry needle, sew facing in place. Sew sleeve seams.

NECKBAND

Place 58 (64) held back neck sts on shorter cir needle, and join MC to beg of sts with RS facing. Work across 58 (64) back neck sts, pick up and knit about 62 (68) sts along cut front neck opening, picking up just below the stitching lines—120 (132) sts. Pm and join for working in the rnd. Work garter st (knit 1 rnd, purl 1 rnd) until neckband measures 2½" (6.5 cm) or desired length, BO all sts.

been completed, place all sts on holders—piece measures about 27½" (70 cm) from lower edging CO.

SLEEVES

With MC and larger straight needles, CO 70 (76) sts. Work in garter st, inc 1 st each end of needle every 4th row 19 (30) times, then every other row 29 (15) times, working incs 1 st in from each edge (do not inc in selvedge sts)—166 sts for both sizes. Work even in garter st until piece measures 17 (19)" (43 [48.5] cm) from CO.

FACING

Change to St st and work ¾" (2 cm) even in St st for facing. BO all sts.

FINISHING
CUT FRONT NECK OPENING

Place center 58 (64) patt panel sts of front and back on separate holders or waste yarn, leaving rem sts at each side on holders for shoulders. Measure down 2½" (6 cm)

knit with MC

• purl with CC

Chart 1

45
43
41
39
37
35
33
31
29
27
25
23
21
19
17
15
13
11
9
7
5
3
1

Chart 2

45
43
41
39
37
35
33
31
29
27
25
23
21
19
17
15
13
11
9
7
5
3
1

Chart 3

45
43
41
39
37
35
33
31
29
27
25
23
21
19
17
15
13
11
9
7
5
3
1

Chart 4

45
43
41
39
37
35
33
31
29
27
25
23
21
19
17
15
13
11
9
7
5
3
1

knit with MC

• purl with CC

Chart 5

Chart 6

KNITTING OUT OF AFRICA

Chart 7

45
43
41
39
37
35
33
31
29
27
25
23
21
19
17
15
13
11
9
7
5
3
1

Chart 8

45
43
41
39
37
35
33
31
29
27
25
23
21
19
17
15
13
11
9
7
5
3
1

Chart 9

45
43
41
39
37
35
33
31
29
27
25
23
21
19
17
15
13
11
9
7
5
3
1

Chart 10

45
43
41
39
37
35
33
31
29
27
25
23
21
19
17
15
13
11
9
7
5
3
1

As in the pullover shown on page 114, the pattern blocks on this vest were inspired by woven and embroidered cloth made by the Shoowa tribe from the Congo. The pattern blocks are smaller than those used for the pullover, but the overall mosaic effect is the same. The lower body of the vest is worked back and forth in garter stitch in one piece that tapers to the waist at both sides, with the selvedges forming the front slit. The upper body is worked in the round to the shoulders with steeks for the armholes and a cut-and-sewn front neck opening that is finished off with a stand-up collar with a short slit at the top. As in the pullover, each two-color pattern is worked in a combination of knit and purl stitches to create a featherstitch effect.

MATERIALS

SIZES 35½ (39½, 44½, 49)" (90 [100.5, 113, 124.5] cm) finished chest/bust circumference. Shown in size 35½" (90 cm).

YARN About 250 (275, 300, 350) g of main color (MC), and 100 (125, 150, 200) g of contrasting color (CC) of fingering-weight (CYCA Super Fine #1) yarn.

Shown here: Isager Highland (100% pure new wool; 612 yd [560 m]/100 g): #14 pine (MC), 3 (3, 3, 4) skeins. Isager Tvinni (100% merino lambswool; 558 yd [510 m]/ 100 g): #7s beige heather (CC), 1 (2, 2, 2) skein(s).

NEEDLES U.S. size 2 (3 mm): 16" (40 cm) and 24" (60 cm) or 32" (80 cm) circular (cir). Adjust needle size if necessary to obtain the correct gauge.

NOTIONS Stitch markers (m); stitch holders; tapestry needle; removable markers or safety pins; sharp-point sewing needle or sewing machine; contrasting basting thread for steeks; matching sewing thread for steeks.

GAUGE 28 sts and 54 rows = 4" (10 cm) in garter st with MC; 29 sts and 33½ rnds = 4" (10 cm) in charted two-color pattern stitch worked in the rnd; each square pattern block for vest front (26 sts and 30 rnds) measures about 3½" (9 cm) square.

NOTES

- Read about stranded two-color knitting on page 96. When working the chart patterns, carry the unused color loosely on the wrong side of the work; strands should never float across the right side of the fabric.
- Beginning and ending points for the Right and Left Diagonal charts are given only once when the charts appear for the first time.
- Because of shaping, the stitch counts of the diagonal pattern sections will change throughout the upper body of the vest. Each time the diagonal patterns begin again after the framing rounds you will need to establish new beginning and ending points. For the back, each time you re-establish the patterns make sure that the Right Diagonal pattern ends at the center pivot-point stitch, and that the Left Diagonal resumes on the other side of the pivot point to form a chevron where the two patterns meet in the middle of the back. For the fronts, make sure that the Right Diagonal ends at the end of the red pattern repeat box, and that the Left Diagonal begins at the start of the red pattern repeat box.

LOWER BODY

With MC and longer cir needle, CO 268 (300, 336, 368) sts.

Row 1: (WS) P1, sl 1 as if to purl (pwise) with yarn in front (wyf), knit to last 2 sts, sl 1 pwise wyf, k1.

Row 2: (RS) P1, knit to end.

Rep the last 2 rows 7 (7, 8, 8) more times—16 (16, 18, 18)

Front Pattern Placement

9	8	7
6	5	4
3	2	1

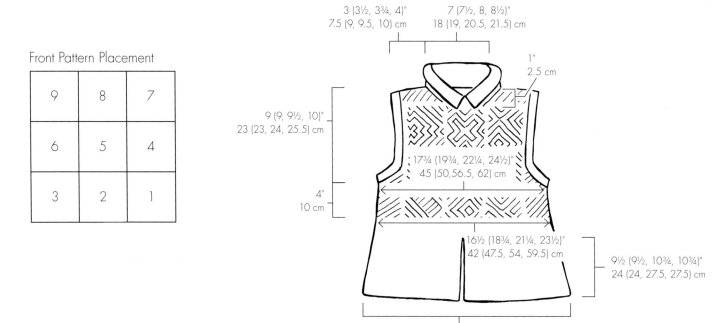

rows; 8 (8, 9, 9) garter ridges completed. Using removable markers or safety pins, place a marker (pm) 67 (75, 84, 92) sts in from each end of needle to indicate position of side "seams"—67 (75, 84, 92) sts each for 2 fronts and 134 (150, 168, 184) sts for back. *Dec row:* (RS) *Knit to 2 sts before marker, k2tog, slip marker (sl m), k2tog; rep from * once more, knit to end—4 sts dec'd. Knit 15 (15, 17, 17) rows. Rep the last 16 (16, 18, 18) rows 6 more times—240 (272, 308, 340) sts rem; 60 (68, 77, 85) sts each for 2 fronts, 120 (136, 154, 170) sts for back; piece measures about 9½ (9½, 10¾, 10¾)" (24 [24, 27.5, 27.5] cm) from CO. Break yarn. Sl the first 60 (68, 77, 85) sts of right front to right-hand needle without working any sts, and pm for beg of rnd; rnd starts at beg of back sts at right side "seam."

UPPER BODY

Note: To the end of the body, work all 2-st sections between the patt blocks in St st (knit every rnd) with MC. Join MC and CC with RS facing. Establish patt and work Rnd 1 of charts (see page 126–127), beg and ending where indicated for your size, as foll: Work 2 sts in St st, 60 (68, 77, 85) sts according to Right Diagonal chart (for back), pm, 58 (66, 75, 83) sts according to Left Diagonal chart (for back), sl m for left side "seam," 2 sts in St st, 16 (24, 33, 41) sts according Right Diagonal chart (for front), 2 sts in St sts, 26 sts according to Chart 1, 2 sts in St st, 26 sts according to Chart 2, 2 sts in St st, 26 sts according to Chart 3, 2 sts in St st, 16 (24, 33, 41) sts according to Left Diagonal chart (for front).

SHAPE SIDES

Side shaping is worked at same time as first tier of pattern blocks; read the next section all the way through before proceeding. Cont in established patt until Rnd 30 of front patt blocks has been completed. *At the same time,* on Rnds 6, 12, 18, and 24 of front patt blocks, inc 1 st at each side of both back and front as foll, working inc'd sts into Left or Right Diagonal patts as established: K2 with MC (right side seam sts), M1 (see Glossary, page 140), work in patt to end of back, M1, k2 with MC (left side seam sts), M1, work in patt to end of front, M1—256 (288, 324, 356) sts after Rnd 24; 128 (144, 162, 178) sts each for back and front. *Framing rnds:* With MC only, knit 3 rnds, repositioning markers on last rnd so markers are in the center of the 2 St sts at each side seam—piece measures about 13½ (13½, 14¾, 14¾)" (34.5 [34.5, 37.5, 37.5] cm) from CO edge, and about 4" (10 cm) from beg of patt.

SHAPE ARMHOLES

Armhole shaping is worked at same time as second and third tiers of patt blocks; read the next section all the way through before proceeding. Establish patt and work Rnd 1 of next tier of charts as foll (see Notes): Ssk (see Glossary, page 140) work 63 (71, 80, 88) sts in Right Diagonal, sl m, 61 (69, 78, 86) sts in Left Diagonal, k2tog, sl left side m, ssk, 19 (27, 36, 44) sts in Right Diagonal, 2 sts in St st, 26 sts according to Chart 4, 2 sts in St sts, 26 sts according to Chart 5, 2 sts in St st, 26 sts according to Chart 6, 2 sts in St st, 19 (27, 36, 44) sts in Left Diagonal, k2tog—4 sts dec'd. Cont in established patt, dec 1 st at each side of both back and front every other rnd 14 more times—196 (228, 264, 296) sts rem; 98 (114, 132, 148) sts each for back and front. Cont to dec 1 st at each side of both back and front every other rnd 2 (4, 10, 14) more times. *At the same time,* knit 3 rnds with MC for framing rnd, then work next tier of patt blocks beg with Rnd 1 of all patt, working Charts 7, 8, and 9 in that order across front, working Left and Right Diagonal patts in established positions, and maintaining St st in MC between patts—188 (212, 224, 240) sts rem when all decs have been completed; 94 (106, 112, 120) sts each for back and front; 3 (9, 12, 16) sts rem in each diagonal patt block at end of front sts. Work even until Rnd 30 of the third tier of blocks has been completed, then knit 3 framing rnds with MC. Establish diagonal patts the same way across both back and front beg with Rnd 1 as foll: *K1 with MC, work 47 (53, 56, 60) sts in right diagonal patt as established, sl m for back or place new marker for front, work 45 (51, 54, 58) sts in left diagonal patt as established, k1 with MC; rep from * once more. Work even in diagonal patt until piece measures 22½ (22½, 24¼, 24¾)" (57 [57, 61.5, 63] cm) from CO edge and armholes measure about 9 (9, 9½, 10)" (23 [23, 24, 25.5] cm), measured straight up along centerline (do not measure along slope of armhole decs).

FINISHING
CUT FRONT NECK OPENING

Place center 50 (54, 58, 62) sts of back and front on separate holders or waste yarn, and place rem 22 (26, 27, 29) sts at each side on holders for shoulders. Measure down to ½" (1.3 cm) above the top of patt Block 8 at center front, or about 1 (1, 1½, 2)" (2.5 [2.5, 3.8, 5] cm) down from sts on holder and place marker. Baste the outline of a rounded front neck opening starting at one edge of the center sts, down to the center front, and back up to the other edge of the center sts. With sewing machine or by hand, sew two lines of small straight stitches along the front basting line. Cut out front neck opening about ¼" (6 mm) inside the basting line to leave a small seam allowance. Back neckline is not shaped; leave 50 (54, 58, 62) back neck sts on holder.

CUT ARMHOLES

Baste a line of contrasting thread along the center of the 2 St sts worked in MC at each side from shoulder to beg of armhole shaping. With sewing machine or by hand, sew a line of small straight stitches one stitch away on each side of the basting line and across the bottom of the armhole. Sew over the same line of stitching again. Carefully cut open the armholes along the basting line from shoulder to base of armholes.

JOIN SHOULDERS

Place about 22 (26, 27, 29) held front shoulder sts on shorter cir needle and about 22 (26, 27, 29) corresponding back shoulder sts on longer cir needle. *Note:* 1 or 2 sts at each cut edge may have been eliminated by the armhole steeks, so you may have fewer shoulder sts available. Turn work carefully inside out, and with right sides touching, use the three-needle bind-off technique (see Glossary, page 140) and the other end of longer cir needle to join shoulders tog. Rep for other shoulder.

ARMHOLE BANDS

With MC, shorter cir needle, and RS facing, pick up and knit 134 (138, 146, 154) sts evenly around armhole. Do not join. Working back and forth in rows, work in garter

st for 10 rows. Change to St st and work even for ¾" (2 cm). BO all sts loosely. Rep for other armhole band.

NECKBAND

Place 50 (54, 58, 62) held back neck sts on shorter cir needle, and join MC to beg of sts with RS facing. Work across 50 (54, 58, 62) back neck sts, pick up and knit about 56 (60, 64, 68) sts along cut front neck opening, picking up just below the stitching lines—106 (114, 122, 130) sts total. Pm and join for working in the rnd. Work garter st (knit 1 rnd, purl 1 rnd) until neckband measures 2" (5 cm) from pick-up rnd, ending with a knit rnd. Break yarn.

Front neck slit: With RS facing, sl 50 (54, 58, 62) back sts and first 28 (30, 32, 34) sts of front without working any sts. Rejoin MC at center front with WS facing. Cont in garter st back and forth in rows, beg and ending at center front for neck slit as foll:

Row 1: (WS) P1, sl 1 pwise wyf, knit to last 2 sts, sl 1 pwise wyf, k1.
Row 2: (RS) P1, knit to end.

Rep the last 2 rows 4 more times, then work WS Row 1 once more—6 garter ridges completed from beg of neck slit; neckband measures about 3" (7.5 cm) from pick-up. With RS facing, BO all sts as if to knit.

Fold armhole bands in half to WS. With yarn threaded on a tapestry needle, sew in place to cover cut edges. Weave in loose ends. Carefully steam-press under a damp cloth.

 knit with MC

 purl with CC

 pattern repeat

Chart 1

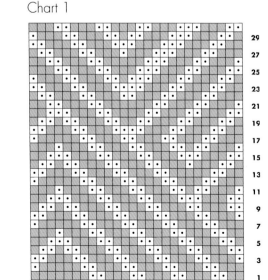

Chart 2

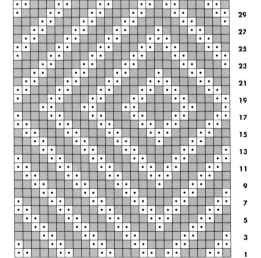

Chart 9

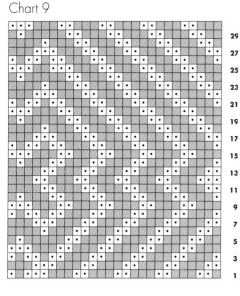

29
27
25
23
21
19
17
15
13
11
9
7
5
3
1

Left Diagonal

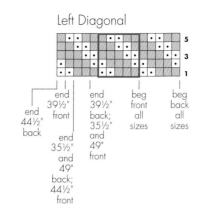

5
3
1

end 44½" back

end 39½" front

end 39½" back; 35½" and 49" front

end 35½" and 49" back; 44½" front

beg front all sizes

beg back all sizes

Right Diagonal

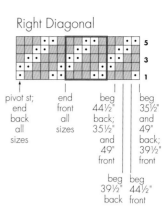

5
3
1

pivot st; end back all sizes

end front all sizes

beg 44½" back; 35½" and 49" front

beg 39½" back

beg 44½" front

beg 35½" and 49" back; 39½" front

Chart 6

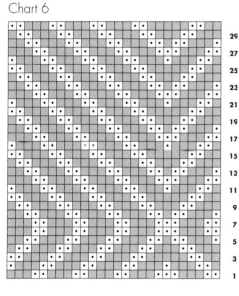

29
27
25
23
21
19
17
15
13
11
9
7
5
3
1

Chart 7

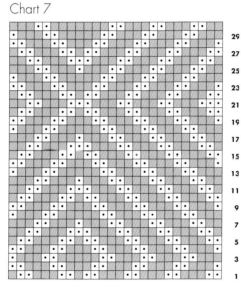

29
27
25
23
21
19
17
15
13
11
9
7
5
3
1

Chart 8

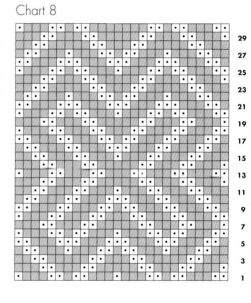

29
27
25
23
21
19
17
15
13
11
9
7
5
3
1

Chart 3

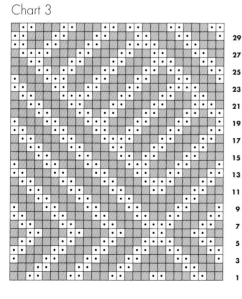

29
27
25
23
21
19
17
15
13
11
9
7
5
3
1

Chart 4

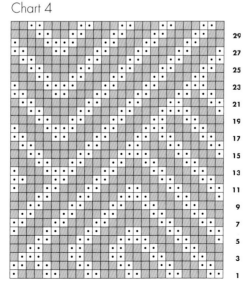

29
27
25
23
21
19
17
15
13
11
9
7
5
3
1

Chart 5

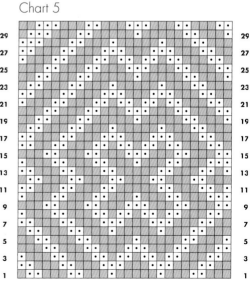

29
27
25
23
21
19
17
15
13
11
9
7
5
3
1

Double knitting is a technique that simultaneously produces two layers of fabric, one light and one dark, with a single pair of needles. The stitches are always worked in pairs, forming two separate stockinette-stitch layers that are worked with separate balls of yarn. One stitch of the pair is worked on the right side; the other stitch is worked on the wrong side. The right side of each layer faces outward and the wrong sides face together and therefore do not show. Reversible patterns form when the yarns for the two layers are interchanged.

The Giraffe and Zebra vests shown on page 130 are worked in double knitting.

PRACTICE DOUBLE KNITTING

To practice double knitting, you will need needles and two balls of yarn; one light and one dark. With both yarns held together, cast on 24 stitches—each stitch will be made up of a light strand and a dark strand. For this example, the light side will be considered the right side of the fabric. Just like stranded two-color knitting (see page 96), the manner in which the yarns are held will result in the stitches of one color being slightly larger than the stitches of the other; the larger stitches are said to be dominant. Work two separate stockinette-stitch layers as follows:

Row 1: (right side facing; the light yarn is dominant) Slip both loops of the first stitch purlwise to form a "linked edge stitch." Hold the two yarns as for stranded two-color knitting (see page 96) with the light strand as the dominant color. *Holding both yarns in back, knit the light loop with the light color (Figure 1), move both yarns to the front of the work and purl the dark loop with the dark color (Figure 2). Repeat from * to the last stitch. Knit the last stitch with both colors held together to form another linked edge stitch—there will be 46 stitches; 2 edge stitches of both colors, 22 light-colored knit stitches, 22 dark-colored purl stitches.

Row 2: (wrong side facing; the dark yarn is dominant) Slip the first stitch purlwise. Hold the two yarns so that the dark strand is the dominant color. *Holding both yarns in back, knit the dark stitch with the dark yarn, move both yarns to the front of the work and purl the light stitch with the light yarn. Repeat from * to the last stitch. Knit the last stitch with both colors held together.

Repeat Rows 1 and 2 until you feel comfortable with the technique.

To interchange the colors to create two-color patterns, simply change the colors that are knitted and purled; i.e., purl the stitches that were previously knitted and knit the stitches that were previously purled. Most double-knitting designs are presented in chart form to show the interaction of the two colors. Charts for double knitting show just one side of the fabric, which we have chosen to call the right side. However, the stitches are always worked in pairs—for example, a knit stitch that is shown as light yarn on a chart is followed by a corresponding dark purl stitch for the wrong side of the fabric, which isn't shown.

SPECIAL TECHNIQUES

Double Knitting Increase: Insert the left needle tip from front to back under the running strand of the front fabric between the two needles, lift the strand onto the left needle, then knit it through the back loop with the front color (Figure 3). Insert the left needle tip from back to front under the running strand of the back fabric between two needles, lift the strand onto the left needle, and purl it through the back loop with the back color—2 new stitches, 1 of each color.

Double Knitting Decrease: Slip the next knit stitch from the left needle to the right needle as if to purl. Slip the purl stitch purlwise onto a spare needle and hold this stitch to the back of the work. Return the slipped knit stitch to the left needle. With both yarns held in back, knit the 2 knit stitches together with the front color (Figure 4). Return the purl stitch from the spare needle to the left needle, and with both yarns held in front, purl the 2 purl stitches together with the back color—1 stitch of each color has been decreased.

Double Knitting Bind Off: With both strands of yarn held together, knit the next 2 stitches together (1 stitch each from front and back face of fabric). *Knit the next 2 stitches together in the same manner—2 stitches on the right needle. Use the left needle tip to lift the first stitch on the right needle up and over the second stitch, and off the needle—1 stitch remains on the right needle; 1 stitch has been bound off. Repeat from * until the required number of stitches has been bound off.

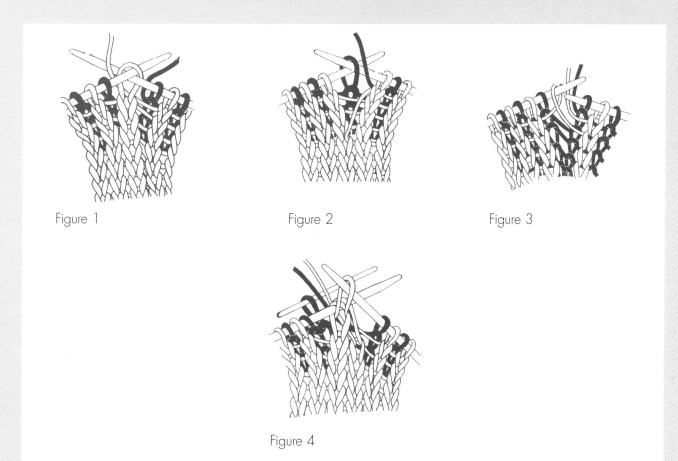

Figure 1

Figure 2

Figure 3

Figure 4

Animals are an integral part of the African landscape. The two vests shown here reflect the markings of the giraffes and zebras that inhabit the grassy plains of Zimbabwe. The bold animal-print designs are worked in reversible double knitting; areas that are dark on the outside of the vest are light on the inside, and vice versa. The Giraffe pullover vest is worked back and forth in rows to shape the asymmetrical lower edge, then continued in the round to the armholes where the piece divides and the front and back are worked separately to the shoulders. The high funnel neck is a playful nod to the vest's namesake. The Zebra V-neck cardigan vest is worked in one piece to the armholes, then divided, and the fronts and back are worked separately to the shoulders.

Natural History Museum, Århus

MATERIALS

SIZES

Giraffe: 37 (42, 46)" (94 (106.5, 117] cm) finished chest/bust circumference. Shown in size 37" (94 cm).

Zebra: 37 (40, 43½)" (94 (101.5, 110.5] cm) finished chest/bust circumference. Shown in size 40" (101.5 cm).

YARN About 85 (95, 110) g each of two colors of fingering-weight (CYCA Super Fine #1) yarn.

Shown here: Isager Tvinni Alpaca (50% lambswool, 50% alpaca, 558 yd [510 m]/100 g).

Giraffe: #30 black and #8s dark brown heather, 1 (1, 2) skein(s) each.

Zebra: #30 black and #0 natural white, 1 (1, 2) skein(s) each.

NEEDLES Vest—U.S. size 2 (3 mm): straight and 24" (60 cm) circular (cir). Edging—U.S. size 1 (2.5 mm) 16" (40 cm) and 24" (60 cm) cir. Adjust needle size if necessary to obtain the correct gauge.

NOTIONS Stitch markers (m); cable needle (cn); tapestry needle.

GAUGE 26 sts and 38 rows = 4" (10 cm) as counted on one face of double knitting using larger needles (see Notes).

STITCH GUIDE
DOUBLE KNITTING

Work the sts in the colors indicated in the directions or on the chart as foll: *With both yarns in back, knit the knit st with one color, then with both yarns in front, purl the purl st with the other color; rep from *.

DOUBLE KNITTING EDGE STITCHES

If edge sts are used they are single sts that are not part of a double knitting knit/purl pair. On every row, slip the first st (edge st) as if to purl with both yarns in front; knit the last st (edge st) with both yarns held tog.

NOTES

• Read about double knitting on page 128. The gauge of double knitting is different from the gauge you might get using the same yarn and needles for single-layer knitting. Choose a section of your chosen chart at least 4" (10 cm) square, preferably larger, for your swatch and block the swatch before measuring to check the gauge. Count only the stitches and rows that are visible on the side of the fabric that faces you.

• The chart shows one face of the double-knitting fabric. Each row on the chart is one row of knitting for both layers. One grid square of the chart represents two stitches on the needle—a knit stitch for the side of the fabric facing towards you (the "front" of the work at that moment), and a purl stitch for the side of the fabric facing away from you (the "back" of the work at that

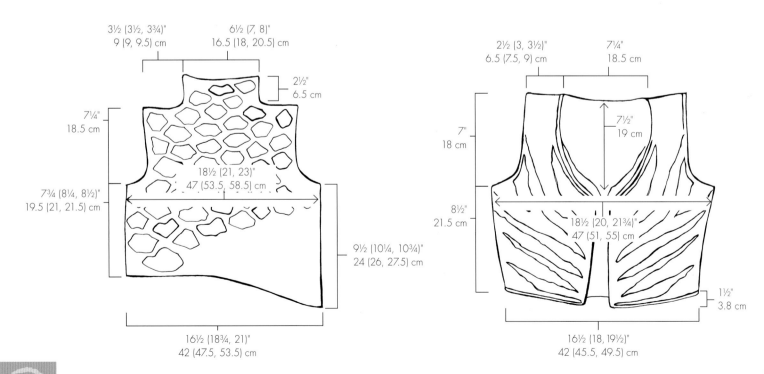

moment). The knit stitch forms the right side of the front fabric, and the purl stitch forms the wrong side of the back fabric.

- For working back and forth in rows, read the odd-numbered rows of the chart from right to left, working the knit stitch of each pair in the color shown on the chart, and the purl stitch in the opposite color. Read the even-numbered rows from left to right, working the knit stitch for each pair in the opposite color, and the purl stitch in the color shown on the chart.
- For working in the round, the same side of fabric will always face you. Read all chart rows from right to left, working the knit stitch of each pair in the color shown on the chart, and the purl stitch in the opposite color.

GIRAFFE

Note
The side with the brown background and black spots is shown on the chart and is referred to in the instructions as the right side; however, the vest can be finished to be reversible.

ASYMMETRICAL LOWER EDGE
With black and larger cir needle, CO 8 sts. Join brown. *Set-up row:* (WS) *With black, knit the first st and leave it on the left needle, bring both yarns to front, purl the same st with brown, sl the st off the left needle, and take both yarns to the back; rep from * 7 more times—16 sts total; 8 knit/purl st pairs.

SHAPE LOWER EDGE
Row 1: (RS) Use the cable method (see Glossary, page 139) to CO 16 sts (8 pairs), alternating black and brown so that last st cast on (first st to be worked) is brown, then work across all sts in double knitting (see Stitch Guide and Notes) in established colors, knitting brown sts and purling black sts—32 sts total; 16 pairs.
Row 2: (WS) Use the cable method to CO 16 sts, alternating brown and black so that last st cast on (first st to be worked) is black, then work across all sts in double knitting as established, knitting the black sts and purling the brown sts—48 sts total; 24 pairs.

Rep the last 2 rows 6 (7, 8) more times—240 (272, 304) sts total; 120 (136, 152) pairs. Cont in double knitting, CO 46 (54, 60) pairs of alternating colors at the beg of the next 2 rows—424 (488, 544) sts, 212 (244, 272) pairs; piece measures about 1¾ (2, 2¼)" (4.5 [5, 5.5] cm) from CO at longer side.

LOWER BODY
Place marker (pm), and join for working in the rnd with brown side as the RS; rnd begins at side of vest. Work 4 (8, 12) rnds even in double knitting, pm in the last rnd after the 106th (122nd, 136th) pair to indicate other side of vest—piece measures about 2 (2¾, 3½)" (5 [7, 9] cm) from CO at longer side. Giraffe chart shows only half the pairs; the vest back and front are worked the same. Establish patt from Rnd 1 of Giraffe chart as foll: *Work 1 pair in patt from chart, inc 1 pair (2 sts inc'd total; see Double Knitting, page 128), work in patt from chart to 1 pair before next m, inc 1 pair, work 1 pair in patt from chart; rep from * once more, working the entire chart again over the sts of the other side—4 pairs inc'd; 108 (124, 138) pairs each for front and back. Cont in patt from chart, inc 1 pair at each side of both front and back every 10 rnds 6 more times, as shown on chart—120 (136, 150) pairs each for front and back; 480 (544, 600) sts total. Work even until Rnd 70 of chart has been completed—piece measures about 9½ (10¼, 10¾)" (24 [26, 27.5] cm) from CO at longer side and 7¾ (8¼, 8½)" (19.5 [21, 21.5] cm) from joining rnd at shorter side.

DIVIDE FOR FRONT AND BACK
(Rnd/Row 71 of chart) BO 4 (6, 8) pairs (see Double Knitting, page 128), work in patt from chart to 4 (6, 8) pairs before next m, BO 8 (12, 16) pairs removing m as you go, work in patt to last 4 (6, 8) pairs, BO rem sts, fasten off last st—112 (124, 134) pairs each for front and back, 224 (248, 268) sts each for front and back. Place sts for back on holder.

UPPER FRONT
Rejoin yarns to front sts with WS (black background) facing, and work Row 72 of chart.

SHAPE ARMHOLES
BO 4 pairs at beg of next 2 rows, then BO 3 pairs at beg of next 2 rows—98 (110, 120) pairs. Dec 1 pair at each side (see Double Knitting, page 128) every row 3 (5, 5)

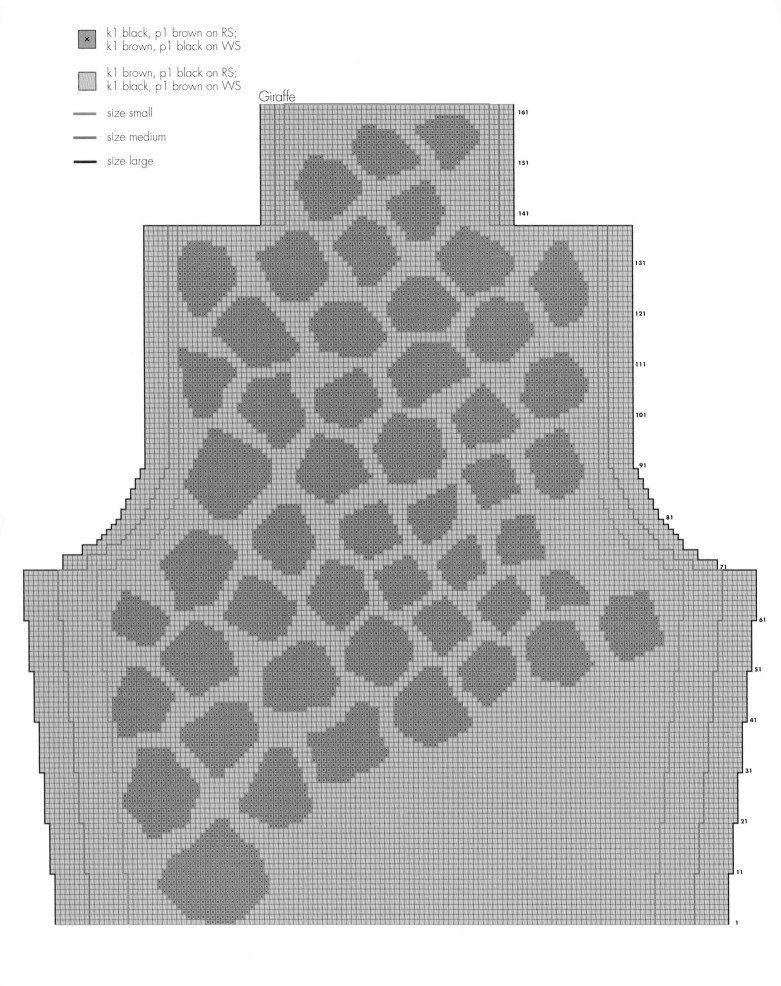

Giraffe

Legend

✗ (dark)	k1 black, p1 brown on RS; k1 brown, p1 black on WS
(light)	k1 brown, p1 black on RS; k1 black, p1 brown on WS

—— size small
—— size medium
—— size large

Row numbers (right edge): 161, 151, 141, 131, 121, 111, 101, 91, 81, 71, 61, 51, 41, 31, 21, 11, 1

times, working dec's 1 pair in from the edge—92 (100, 110) pairs. Dec 1 pair at each side every other row 3 (5, 5) times—86 (90, 100) pairs rem. Work even until Row 138 of chart has been completed—armholes measure about 7¼" (18.5) cm. Place sts on holder.

UPPER BACK

Return 112 (124, 134) held pairs for back to needle. Rejoin yarns with WS (black background) facing, and work Row 72 of chart. Complete as for front, and place sts on holder.

JOIN SHOULDERS

Place center 42 (46, 52) pairs for front and back on separate holders—22 (22, 24) shoulder pairs rem at each side. Arrange one set of front shoulder sts on two straight needles, with the brown sts on one needle and the black sts on the other. Place sts for the corresponding back shoulder on two more straight needles in same way. Hold the two needles with the brown sts so that the right sides (brown background) of the piece are touching. With brown, use the three-needle bind-off technique (see Glossary, page 140) to join brown sts of shoulder. Hold the two needles with the black sts with wrong sides touching, and use the three-needle bind-off technique to join black sts of shoulder; black BO forms a decorative welt that will show on the public side if you wear the vest with the black background on the outside.

FINISHING
NECKBAND

Place the 42 (46, 52) held pairs each from front and back on larger straight needle—84 (92, 104) pairs. Join yarns with RS facing. Work Row 139 of chart, inc a single st at each end of needle for edge sts—84 (92, 104) pairs, 2 edge sts (not shown on chart). Work back and forth in rows (do not join into a rnd), working neck section of chart twice across neck pairs, and working 1 st at each end as double knitting edge st (see Stitch Guide). When Row 162 has been completed, BO all sts using black only. Join second shoulder same as the first, leaving side of neckband open.

LOWER EDGING

With black, smaller 24" (60 cm) cir needle, and RS facing, pick up and knit about 214 (244, 272) sts around lower opening—about 26 sts for every 4" (10 cm) around edge; exact st count is not critical. Work in regular single-layer St st for 6 rows. BO all sts. Turn edging to WS, and sew securely in place with yarn threaded on a tapestry needle as invisibly as possible so that vest is reversible.

ARMHOLE EDGING

With black, smaller 16" (40 cm) cir needle, and RS facing, pick up and knit about 126 (132, 140) sts around armhole. Complete as for lower edging.

Weave in loose ends. Lightly steam-press.

ZEBRA

Notes

The side with the black background and white stripes is shown on the chart and is referred to in the instructions as the right side; however, the vest can be finished to be reversible.

For the right front, work the Zebra chart from the center front opening to the side of the garment on RS rows and from the side to center front opening on WS rows. For the left front, work from the side of the garment to the center front opening on RS rows, and from the center front opening to the side on WS rows. For back, work across the entire chart, reading RS rows from right to left, and WS rows from left to right; work the center back st (not shown) in color to match the sts on either side.

SHAPED LOWER FRONTS
RIGHT LOWER FRONT

With black and larger straight needles, CO 10 sts. Join white. *Set-up row:* (WS) *With white, knit the first st and leave it on the left needle, bring both yarns to front, purl the same st with black, sl the st off the left needle, and take both yarns to the back; rep from * 8 more times, knit last st with both yarns held together (edge st, not shown on chart)—19 sts total; 9 knit/purl st pairs, 1 edge st. Work the single edge st at center front opening as double knitting edge st throughout (see Stitch Guide, page 132). Work Row 1 of Zebra chart (see page 136) for right front point in established colors (see Stitch Guide and Notes), knitting black sts and purling white sts. *Next row:* (WS; Row 2 of chart) Use the cable method (see Glossary, page 139) to CO 18 sts (9 pairs), alternating black and white so that last st cast on (first st to be worked) is white, work to last st in double knitting as established (knitting the white sts and purling the black sts), work edge st—37 sts

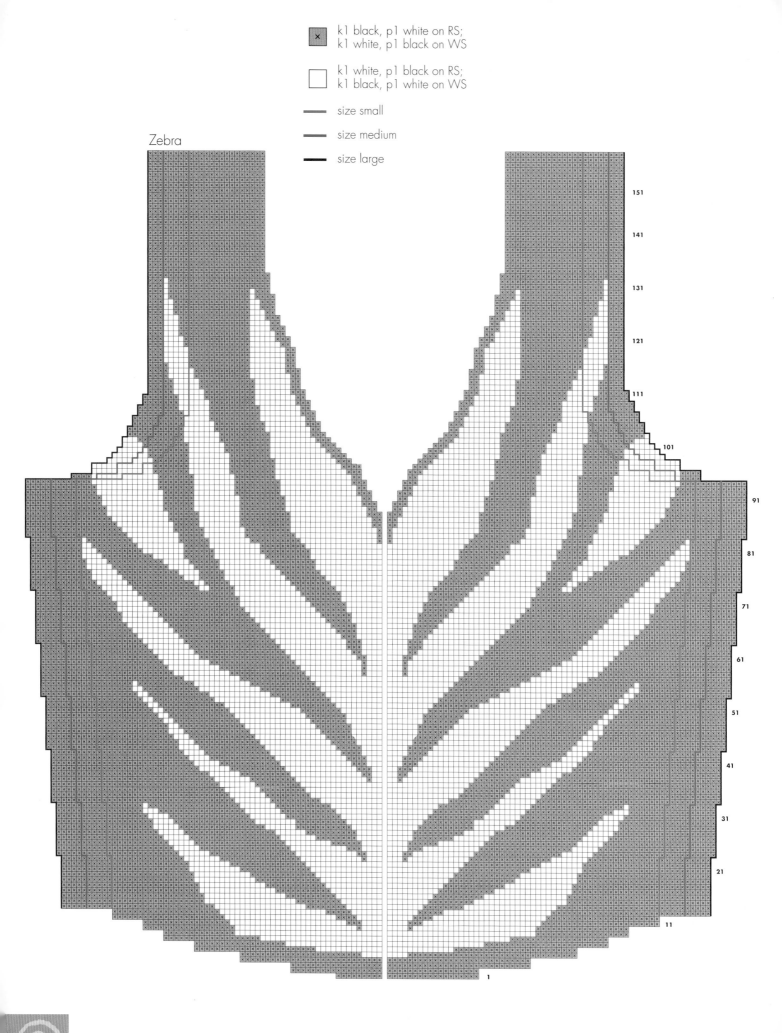

Zebra

☒	k1 black, p1 white on RS; k1 white, p1 black on WS
☐	k1 white, p1 black on RS; k1 black, p1 white on WS
—	size small
—	size medium
—	size large

151

141

131

121

111

101

91

81

71

61

51

41

31

21

11

1

total; 18 pairs, 1 edge st. Cont in patt from chart, CO 10 pairs at beg of chart Row 4, CO 9 pairs at beg of Row 6, CO 6 pairs at beg of Row 8, CO 4 pairs at beg of Row 10, CO 6 pairs at beg of Row 12, and CO 0 (5, 10) pairs at beg of Row 14—53 (58, 63) pairs; 107 (117, 127) sts total, including edge st. Place sts on holder.

LEFT LOWER FRONT

With black and larger straight needles, CO 10 sts. Join white. *Set-up row:* (WS) Knit first st with both yarns held together (edge st; not shown on chart), *with white, knit the first st and leave it on the needle, bring both yarns to front and purl the same st with black, sl the st off the left needle, and take both yarns to the back; rep from * 8 more times—19 sts total; 9 knit/purl st pairs, 1 edge st. Work the single edge st at center front opening as double knitting edge st throughout (see Stitch Guide). *Next row:* (RS; Row 1 of chart) Use the cable method to CO 18 sts (9 pairs), alternating black and white so that last st cast on (first st to be worked) is black, work to last st in double knitting as established (knitting the black sts and purling the white sts), work edge st—37 sts total; 18 pairs, 1 edge st. Cont in patt from chart, CO 10 pairs at beg of chart Row 3, CO 9 pairs at beg of Row 5, CO 6 pairs at beg of Row 7, CO 4 pairs at beg of Row 9, CO 6 pairs at beg of Row 11, and CO 0 (5, 10) pairs at beg of Row 13—53 (58, 63) pairs; 107 (117, 127) sts total, including edge st. Work Row 14 of chart even. Place sts on holder.

LOWER BODY

Transfer both sets of front sts to larger cir needle with RS facing and right front sts as the first sts group of sts to be worked. Join yarns. *Joining row:* Work 1 edge st, work Row 15 of chart across right front sts, place marker (pm), using the backward loop method (see Glossary, page 139) CO 214 (234, 254) sts with black and white alternately to create 107 (117, 127) pairs for back, pm, work Row 15 of chart across left front sts, work 1 edge st—213 (233, 253) pairs, 2 edge sts; 428 (468, 508) sts total. Cont in patt from chart until Row 23 has been completed. On Row 24, inc at sides as foll: *Work in patt to 1 st pair before side marker (m), inc 1 pair (2 sts inc'd total; see Double Knitting Increase, page 128), work 2 pairs in patt, slipping side m, inc 1 pair; rep from * once more—4 pairs inc'd; 54 (59, 64) pairs for each front, 109 (119, 129) pairs for back, 2 edge sts. Cont in patt from chart, inc 2 pairs at each side in this manner every 10 rnds 6 more times as shown

on chart—60 (65, 70) pairs for each front, 121 (131, 141) pairs for back, 2 edge sts; 484 (524, 564) sts total. Work even until Row 88 of chart has been completed.

SHAPE FRONT NECK

(Row 89 of chart) Dec 1 pair at each end of row (see Double Knitting Decrease, page 129), working decs 1 pair in from edge sts—2 pairs dec'd. Cont in patt from chart until Row 94 has been completed, cont neck shaping shown on chart—57 (62, 67) pairs rem for each front, 121 (131, 141) pairs for back, 2 edge sts; piece measures about 10" (25.5 cm) from CO of fronts, and 8½" (21.5 cm) from CO for back.

DIVIDE FOR FRONTS AND BACK

(Row 95 of chart) Cont neck shaping (i.e., dec 1 pair at each front neck), work in patt to last 9 pairs of right front, BO 18 pairs (removing side m as you go), work in patt to last 9 pairs of back, BO 18 pairs, work to end of left front—47 (52, 57) pairs for each front, 103 (113, 123) pairs for back, 2 edge sts. Place sts for back and right front on holders.

LEFT FRONT

Cont to dec at neck edge as shown on chart, work 1 WS row even.

SHAPE ARMHOLE

Cont neck shaping, BO 4 pairs at beg of next RS row, then BO 3 pairs at beg of foll RS row. Cont neck shaping, dec 1 pair at armhole every row 3 times, working dec's 1 pair in from the edge, then dec 1 pair at armhole every other row 3 (3, 5) times. When all shaping for neck and armhole has been completed, 15 (20, 23) pairs and 1 edge st rem. Work even until Row 158 of chart has been completed—armhole measures about 7" (18) cm. Place sts on holder.

RIGHT FRONT

Return 47 (52, 57) held pairs for right front to needle. Rejoin yarns with WS facing.

SHAPE ARMHOLE

Cont neck shaping, BO 4 pairs at beg of next WS row, then BO 3 pairs at beg of foll WS row. Cont neck shaping, dec 1 pair at armhole every row 3 times, then dec 1 pair at armhole every other row 3 (3, 5) times—15 (20, 23) pairs and 1 edge st rem when all neck and armhole shaping has been completed. Work even until Row 158 of chart has been completed—armhole measures about 7" (18) cm. Place sts on holder.

BACK
Return 103 (113, 123) held pairs for back to needle. Rejoin yarns with WS facing.

SHAPE ARMHOLES
BO 4 pairs at the beg of next 2 rows, then BO 3 pairs at beg of foll 2 rows—89 (99, 109) pairs rem. Dec 1 pair at each end of needle every row 3 times, then dec 1 pair at each end of needle every other row 3 (3, 5) times—77 (87, 93) pairs rem. Work even until Row 158 of chart has been completed—armhole measures about 7" (18) cm. Place center 47 pairs on one holder for back neck, and place 15 (20, 23) pairs for each shoulder on separate holders.

JOIN SHOULDERS
Arrange one set of front shoulder sts on two straight needles, with the black sts on one needle and the white sts on the other. Place sts for the corresponding back shoulder on two more straight needles in same way. Hold the two needles with the white sts so that the wrong sides (white background) of the piece are touching. With white, use the three-needle bind-off technique (see Glossary, page 140) to join white sts of shoulder. Hold the two needles with the black sts with wrong sides touching, and use the three-needle bind-off techinque to join black sts of shoulder;

black BO forms a decorative welt that will show on the public side if you wear the vest with the black background on the outside. Join second shoulder the same way.

FINISHING
LOWER EDGING
With black, smaller 24" (60 cm) cir needle, and RS facing, pick up and knit about 214 (234, 254) sts around lower edge—about 26 sts for every 4" (10 cm) around edge; exact st count is not critical. Work in regular single-layer St st for 6 rows. BO all sts. Turn edging to WS, and sew securely in place with yarn threaded on a tapestry needle as invisibly as possible so that vest is reversible.

ARMHOLE EDGING
With black, smaller 16" (40 cm) cir needle, and RS facing, pick up and knit about 122 (128, 136) sts around armhole. BO all sts. Complete as for lower edging.

NECK EDGING
With black, smaller 24" (60 cm) cir needle, RS facing, and beg at lower right front, pick up and knit about 110 sts along right front opening to shoulder, work k2tog 47 times across held back neck sts to convert sts from double knitting to single knitting, pick up and knit about 110 sts along left front edge—267 sts; exact st count is not critical. Complete as for lower edging.

Weave in loose ends. Lightly steam-press.

Poul Valsted

ABBREVIATIONS

beg	beginning; begin; begins		rem	remain(s); remaining
bet	between		rep	repeat
BO	bind off		rev St st	reverse stockinette stitch
CC	contrasting color		rib	ribbing
cm	centimeter(s)		rnd(s)	round(s)
cn	cable needle		RS	right side
CO	cast on		sl	slip
cont	continue(s); continuing		sl st	slip stitch (sl 1 stitch pwise
dec(s)	decrease(s); decreasing			unless otherwise indicated)
dpn	double-pointed needle(s)		ssk	slip 1 kwise, slip 1 kwise, k2 slipped
foll	following; follows			stitches together tbl (decrease)
g	grams		ssp	slip 1 kwise, slip 1 kwise, p2 slipped
inc	increase(s); increasing			stitches together tbl (decrease)
k	knit		st(s)	stitch(es)
k1f&b	knit into front and back of same stitch		St st	stockinette stitch
k2tog	knit two stitches together		tbl	through back loop
kwise	knitwise		tog	together
LC	left cross		WS	wrong side
m(s)	marker(s)		wyb	with yarn in back
MC	main color		wyf	with yarn in front
mm	millimeters		yo	yarn over
M1	make one (increase)		*	repeat starting point
p	purl			(i.e., repeat from *)
p1f&b	purl into front and back of same stitch		* *	repeat all instructions
p2tog	purl two stitches together			between asterisks
patt(s)	pattern(s)		( )	alternate measurements
pm	place marker			and/or instructions
psso	pass slipped stitch over		[ ]	alternate measurements or instructions
p2sso	pass two slipped stitches over			that are to be worked as a group
pwise	purlwise			a specified number of times
RC	right cross			

YARN SOURCES

All Isager yarns used in this book, as well as kits of the projects, are available in the United States from:

NORDIC FIBER ARTS
Four Cutts Road
Durham, NH 03824-3101
(603) 868-1196
www.nordicfiberarts.com
info@nordicfiberarts.com

Isager Highland
100% pure new wool
612 yards (560 meters)/100 grams

Isager Spinni
100% pure new wool
667 yards (610 meters)/100 grams

Isager Tvinni
100% merino lambswool
558 yards (510 meters)/100 grams

Isager Tvinni Alpaca
50% lambswool, 50% alpaca
558 yards (510 meters)/100 grams

GLOSSARY

CONTINENTAL (LONG-TAIL) CAST-ON

Leaving a long tail (about ½" to 1" [1.3 to 2.5 cm] for each stitch to be cast on), make a slipknot and place on right needle. Place thumb and index finger of left hand between yarn ends so that working yarn is around index finger and tail end is around thumb. Secure ends with your other fingers and hold palm upwards, making a V of yarn (Figure 1). Bring needle up through loop on thumb (Figure 2), grab first strand around index finger with needle, and go back down through loop on thumb (Figure 3). Drop loop off thumb and, placing thumb back in V configuration, tighten resulting stitch on needle (Figure 4).

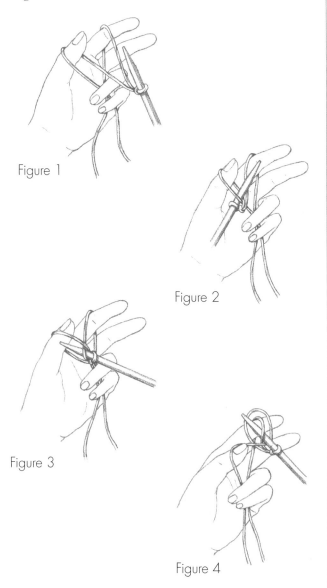

Figure 1

Figure 2

Figure 3

Figure 4

KNITTED CAST-ON

Place slipknot on left needle if there are no established stitches. *With right needle, knit into first stitch (or slipknot) on left needle (Figure 1) and place new stitch onto left needle (Figure 2). Repeat from *, always knitting into last stitch made.

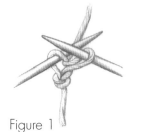
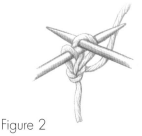

Figure 1

Figure 2

CABLE CAST-ON

Begin with a slipknot and one knitted cast-on stitch if there are no established stitches. *Insert right needle between first two stitches on left needle (Figure 1). Wrap yarn as if to knit. Draw yarn through to complete stitch (Figure 2) and slip this new stitch to left needle as shown (Figure 3). Repeat from *, always working between the first two stitches on left needle.

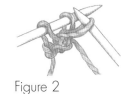

Figure 1

Figure 2

Figure 3

BACKWARD LOOP CAST-ON

*Loop working yarn and place it on needle backward so that it doesn't unwind. Repeat from *.

RAISED (M1) INCREASES

Left Slant (**M1L**): With left needle tip, lift strand between needles from front to back (Figure 1). Knit lifted loop through the back (Figure 2).

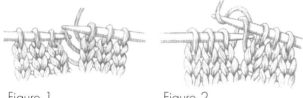

Figure 1   Figure 2

Right Slant (**M1R**): With left needle tip, lift strand between needles from back to front (Figure 1). Knit lifted loop through the front (Figure 2).

Figure 1   Figure 2

Purlwise (**M1P**): With left needle tip, lift strand between needles, from back to front (Figure 1). Purl lifted loop (Figure 2).

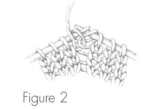

Figure 1   Figure 2

BAR INCREASE (K1F&B)

Knit into a stitch and leave it on the left needle (Figure 1), then knit through the back loop of the same stitch (Figure 2). There will be two stitches made from one (Figure 3).

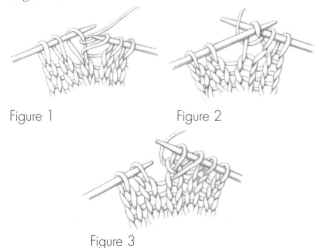

Figure 1   Figure 2

Figure 3

SSK DECREASE

Slip two stitches knitwise one at a time onto right needle (Figure 1). Insert point of left needle into front of two slipped stitches and knit them together through back loops with right needle (Figure 2).

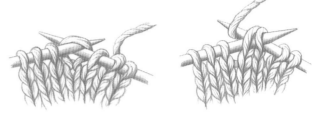

Figure 1   Figure 2

SSSK: Work as for ssk, but slip three stitches knitwise, then knit them together through their back loops.

SSP DECREASE

Holding yarn in front, slip two stitches knitwise one at a time onto right needle (Figure 1). Slip them back onto left needle and purl the two stitches together through their back loops (Figure 2).

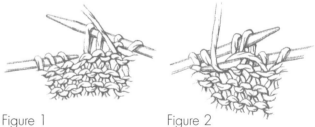

Figure 1   Figure 2

THREE-NEEDLE BIND-OFF

Place stitches to be joined onto two separate needles. Hold them with right sides of knitting facing together. Insert a third needle into first stitch on each of the other two needles and knit them together as one stitch. *Knit next stitch on each needle the same way. Pass first stitch over second stitch. Repeat from * until one stitch remains on third needle. Cut yarn and pull tail through last stitch.

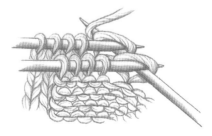

MATTRESS STITCH SEAM

With right side of knitting facing, use threaded needle to pick up one bar between first two stitches on one piece (Figure 1), then pick up corresponding bar plus the bar above it on other piece (Figure 2). *Pick up next two bars on first piece, then next two bars on the other (Figure 3). Repeat from * to end of seam, finishing by picking up last bar (or pair of bars) at the top of first piece.

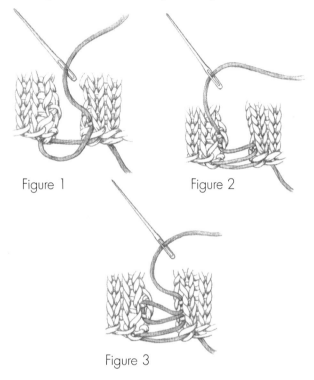

Figure 1   Figure 2

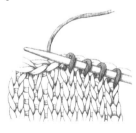

Figure 3

PICK UP AND KNIT STITCHES

Along bind-off edge: With right side facing and working from right to left, *insert needle tip into center of stitch below bind-off edge (Figure 1), wrap yarn around needle, and pull it through (Figure 2). Repeat from *.

Figure 1   Figure 2

Along shaped edge: With right side facing and working from right to left, *insert needle tip between last and second-to-last stitches, wrap yarn around needle, and pull it through. Repeat from *, picking up about three stitches for every four rows, unless otherwise instructed.

Figure 1

Pick up and purl: With wrong side facing and working from right to left, *insert needle tip under selvedge stitch from the far side to the near side, wrap yarn around needle purlwise (Figure 1), and pull it through (Figure 2). Repeat from *.

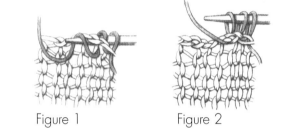

Figure 1   Figure 2

ZIPPER

With right side facing and zipper closed, pin zipper to fronts so front edges cover the zipper teeth. With contrasting thread and RS facing, baste zipper in place close to teeth (Figure 1). Turn work over and with matching sewing thread and needle, stitch outer edges of zipper to wrong side of fronts (Figure 2), being careful to follow a single column of sts in the knitting to keep zipper straight. Turn work back to right side facing, and with matching sewing thread, sew knitted fabric close to teeth (Figure 3). Remove basting.

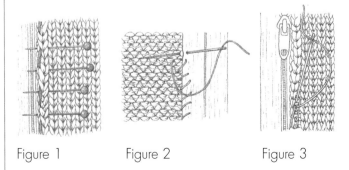

Figure 1   Figure 2   Figure 3

INDEX